Win-Win
Performance Appraisals

Win-Win
Performance Appraisals

**Get the Best Results for Yourself and Your Employees:
What to Do Before, During, and After the Review**

Lawrence Holpp

McGraw-Hill

New York Chicago San Francisco Lisbon
London Madrid Mexico City Milan New Delhi
San Juan Seoul Singapore Sydney Toronto

The *McGraw·Hill* Companies

1 2 3 4 5 6 7 8 9 0 DOC/DOC 1 6 5 4 3 2 1

ISBN   978-0-07-173611-4
MHID   0-07-173611-5

e-ISBN 978-0-07-173985-6
e-MHID   0-07-173985-8

This is a CWL Publishing Enterprises book developed for McGraw-Hill by CWL Publishing Enterprises, Inc., Madison, Wisconsin, www.cwlpub.com.

Product or brand names used in this book may be trade names or trademarks. Where we believe there may be proprietary claims to such trade names or trademarks, the name has been used with an initial capital or it has been capitalized in the style used by the name claimant. Regardless of the capitalization used, all such names have been used in an editorial manner without any intent to convey endorsement of or other affiliation with the name claimant. Neither the author nor the publisher intends to express any judgment as to the validity or legal status of any such proprietary claims.

McGraw-Hill books are available at special quantity discounts to use as premiums and sales promotions, or for use in corporate training programs. To contact a representative, please e-mail us at bulksales@mcgraw-hill.com.

This book is printed on acid-free paper.

Contents

Acknowledgments   xi

Introduction   xiii
What Is Your Situation?
The Purpose of Performance Appraisal
Perfect Performance Appraisal

1. What's Your Situation?   1
Performance Management in Your Organization   1
Performance Management: Six Assumptions   4
Performance Management Cycle   5
Organization of This Book   6

2. Setting Objectives   7
The Manager's Role in Setting Objectives   8
    Set Objectives for Your Work Group   8
The Employee's Role in Setting Objectives   9
Inputs into the Objective-Setting Process   10
    Strategic Corporate Goals   10
    Work Unit Objectives   11
    Position Descriptions   11
    Objectives from Prior Appraisals   13
    Input from Others   13
    Personal Development   15
Developing Objectives   15

Criteria for Effective Objectives   16
Meetings to Discuss Progress Toward Objectives   18

3. Improving on Performance Appraisal Forms   **21**
Completing the Objectives Section   22
   Using the 4Ws and 1H to Turn Goals into Objectives   *22*
Turning Competencies into Objectives   24
   Using Action Verbs   *26*
Working with Final Ratings   27
   Behaviorally Anchored Rating Scale   *28*
   Competencies with Descriptors and Behavioral Indicators   *31*
Another Dimension of Performance—Potential   31
   Performance and Potential: Options for Coaching
      and Development   *31*
Technology and Performance Appraisals   40

4. Evaluating Your Employees   **43**
Schedule the Meeting and Prepare Your Employee   44
Decide on Your Approach   46
Evaluate Your Employee   47
   Begin with the Best   *47*
   Review the Evaluation Period   *48*
   Rate the Performance   *49*
   Sources of Bias in Evaluations   *49*
   Maintain Balance   *53*
   Narratives   *53*
Prepare for the Meeting   55
   Make a Plan   *55*
   Plan Your Opening   *56*
   Anticipate Reactions   *57*
   Prepare to Ask Questions   *58*
   Review Development Needs   *61*

5. Conducting Performance Appraisal Meetings   **65**
Preliminaries   65
Beginning the Meeting   67
Discussing the Evaluation   68
   Starting with the Bottom Line   *69*
   Going Item by Item   *69*
   Asking Questions   *72*
   Listening   *73*
   Dealing with Emotions   *74*

    Disagreeing 75
    Diagnosing Difficulties 77
  Final Matters 78
    Closing the Meeting 78
    Following Up 79

6. Legal Issues in Performance Management **81**
  A Little Common Sense 81
    Take Precautions with Procedures 82
    Focus on Job Performance 82
    Treat Your Employees Equally 83
    Conduct Performance Appraisals at Least Annually 83
    Put It in Writing 84
    Communicate with Your Employees 85
    Keep Employee Records Confidential 85
    It's Tough, but It's Your Responsibility 85
    Don't Set Employees Up to Fail 86
  Discrimination 87
  Other Legal Issues 89
  Final Words of Advice 90

7. Following Up After the Performance Appraisal Meeting **95**
  Reacting to Good Performance 97
    Reward vs. Recognition 97
    Rewards 98
    Recognition 99
    The Most Important Rule of Rewards and Recognition 101
    Abraham Maslow and Frederick Herzberg 102
    Pay for Performance 106
  Performance Diagnosis 108
    Approaches and Tools 109
    Causes and Possible Solutions 112
    "The System" 118
    Diagnosing Success 119
    Serious Attitude Problems 120
    Continuous Performance Diagnosis 123
  Performance Improvement Planning 123
  Performance Planning 125
    Improve Job Descriptions 127
  Personal Development Planning 127
  Performance Appraisal Responsibilities of Your Employees 129
    Closure and Overture 130

8. Performance Management as a Continuous Process   **131**
Schedule Your Commitments   131
Continue the Process of Diagnosis and Improvement   132
Coaching Your Employees   133
  What Is Coaching?   *133*
  What Makes Coaching Effective?   *135*
  Personal Issues   *136*
  Delivering Doses of Coaching   *137*
Observing Your Employees   137
Communicating with Your Employees   138
  Importance of Being Open to Communication   *140*
  Perceiving and Processing and Thinking and Behaving   *140*
Motivating Your Employees   143
  In General   *143*
  As Individuals   *144*
Guiding Your Employees   145
  Asking the Right Questions and Asking Questions Right   *145*
  Listening   *148*
Using Feedback with Your Employees   150
  Providing Feedback   *150*
  Getting Feedback   *152*
Action Steps for Coaching Something New   154
Monitoring Your Employees' Progress   155
Coaching in Sessions   156
  Documenting Coaching Sessions   *158*
  Applying a Little Pressure   *161*
Dealing with Employee Problems   162
Appraise Your Performance as Coach   164

9. Managing Teams and Performance Appraisal   **167**
In the Beginning   167
  Performance Appraisal   *168*
  For Example   *168*
  Assessing Team Development   *170*
  Assessing Team Behavior   *171*
  Assessing Member Behavior   *173*
Stages of Team Development   174
Performance Appraisal of Individual Team Members   176
  Team-Centered Performance Review   *176*
Recognize and Reward Team Achievements ...   177
  ... and Each Individual   *177*

A Final Word	179
Index	181

Acknowledgments

I would like to thank John Woods of CWL Publishing Enterprises for recruiting me to work on this book. And I owe a big debt of gratitude to Robert Magnan who did a great job of editing and helping me create the final manuscript. He had a lot to do with the creation of the book you now hold. Thanks Bob.

Introduction

With few exceptions, both managers and employees dread appraisal time. Managers are afraid of demotivating employees by giving them critical feedback and employees are afraid of receiving negative feedback that may threaten their jobs and even their careers. Both managers and employees may consider the process a waste of time and energy.

Performance appraisals are also expensive. Consider all the hours that a manager spends in planning, executing, and following up on performance appraisals. Consider the impact on each employee: the time spent thinking and talking about an upcoming appraisal, the time spent with his or her manager, the time spent thinking about the appraisal session and talking about it with other employees, and the loss in productivity and morale when the results are not good.

Performance appraisals can work. They can help organizations maintain focus on their strategic plan. They can enable managers to assess the performance of their employees. They can help employees know how well they are doing their jobs. They can provide a more solid basis for decisions on pay raises, promotions, and terminations.

What Is Your Situation?

If you're reading this book, chances are you're a manager who is required by your company to do performance appraisals on your employees. You may have had some training in doing them, but you are still a little uncertain about your ability to do them successfully without alienating your employees or getting into hot water. You may not have much experience in conducting appraisals, although you may have been subjected to many of them. Maybe you are new to managerial responsibilities. Or maybe you've just recently found out that you're expected to do performance appraisals. Maybe you have done lots of performance appraisals. A key quality of any manager should be an interest in managing more effectively and more efficiently. It's even possible that you're not required to do performance appraisals, but you think it's a good idea. That's smart, for the benefits for performance management and for the protection against legal liabilities.

Whatever your situation, helping you manage performance appraisals better is the purpose of this book.

The Purpose of Performance Appraisal

Performance appraisal is not about filling out a form. It's not even about having a performance appraisal meeting. It's about managing performance. Performance management is the larger heading under which performance appraisal falls, along with coaching, career development, compensation, feedback, objective setting, performance planning, mentoring, and employee engagement.

Performance appraisal is one tool among many that can help a manager lead his or her employees to achieve results consistent with the goals of the organization and their business unit. If it's the only tool employed, it will feel like a blunt instrument. If it's used

Working Definition: Performance Management
The process by which management drives overall strategic objectives and goals into day-to-day goals and actions that translate into measurable results that improve business success.

in concert with the other tools in the box, performance appraisal can become a highly effective means to do the following:

- Improve manager-employee communication
- Promote better work performance
- Help employees develop their potential
- Ensure that team members are working together to achieve results
- Initiate a measurement system that ensures equitable decisions
- Provide a sound basis for all employment decisions from hiring to firing

The performance management process ensures that businesses approach their people strategy with as much rigor as they do their business strategy.

Ongoing dialogue and feedback enable associates to develop and grow while having line of sight to their impact on business results.

The most important aspect of this process is not a tool or a methodology, but rather *the two-way dialogue and the learning that comes from the discussions about areas of success, improvement, and the actions and focus needed to drive additional success.*

Each associate and manager needs to be an active participant in these discussions so there is clarity on what is needed to maximize productivity and success.

Perfect Performance Appraisal

But to achieve this kind of impact and to have access to all the tools in the performance management toolbox, a manager must understand the whole picture of what it takes for the perfect performance appraisal.

Managers and employees need not dread appraisals—not if they are done well, with respect, with skill, and with dignity. The perfect appraisal is not a single one-hour event. Instead, it's a process in which manager and employee plan and work together to achieve their goals and a sense of greater satisfaction.

The purpose of this book is to lay out that strategy from the beginning—setting great objectives—to the end—the perfect appraisal.

> **Working Definition: The Perfect Appraisal**
> The perfect appraisal is one that is tightly linked to the organization's strategy while using the employee's skills, experience, and goals in a way that provides a sense of satisfaction and achievement for both the employee and the manager.

In a sense, a perfect appraisal is the one that almost doesn't need to happen because manager and employee are so aligned on goals and standards that they both understand and agree on the direction and thrust of work from day to day.

But that's in a perfect world. In this world, we do the best that we can. It takes work and planning. The purpose of this book is to help you invest your time and energy more effectively, aiming your efforts toward the goal of the perfect performance appraisal.

Win-Win
Performance Appraisals

1 | What's Your Situation?

What performance management and appraisal mean in your specific situation depends at least largely on your organization and on expectations—both formal and informal, explicit and implied.

What is performance management for your organization? How is it handled? What are the processes and practices?

Performance Management in Your Organization

There are several models for *performance management maturity* that show a progression consisting of four or five stages or levels. Exhibit 1-1 shows an example of a performance management maturity model.

In the Performance Management Maturity Model (PMMM) (Exhibit 1-1), roughly one-third of organizations are stuck in Stage 0 or 1. These are typically, but not solely, small businesses that need some sort of performance appraisal form to protect themselves from lawsuits arising from claims of improper action by their managers. The performance appraisal process is not taken too seriously. Distribution and collection of forms are the responsibil-

Win-Win Performance Appraisals

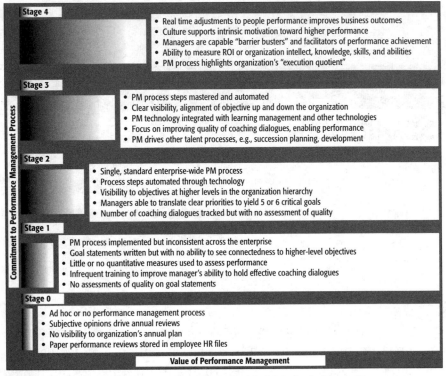

Stage 4
- Real time adjustments to people performance improves business outcomes
- Culture supports intrinsic motivation toward higher performance
- Managers are capable "barrier busters" and facilitators of performance achievement
- Ability to measure ROI or organization intellect, knowledge, skills, and abilities
- PM process highlights organization's "execution quotient"

Stage 3
- PM process steps mastered and automated
- Clear visibility, alignment of objective up and down the organization
- PM technology integrated with learning management and other technologies
- Focus on improving quality of coaching dialogues, enabling performance
- PM drives other talent processes, e.g., succession planning, development

Stage 2
- Single, standard enterprise-wide PM process
- Process steps automated through technology
- Visibility to objectives at higher levels in the organization hierarchy
- Managers able to translate clear priorities to yield 5 or 6 critical goals
- Number of coaching dialogues tracked but with no assessment of quality

Stage 1
- PM process implemented but inconsistent across the enterprise
- Goal statements written but with no ability to see connectedness to higher-level objectives
- Little or no quantitative measures used to assess performance
- Infrequent training to improve manager's ability to hold effective coaching dialogues
- No assessments of quality on goal statements

Stage 0
- Ad hoc or no performance management process
- Subjective opinions drive annual reviews
- No visibility to organization's annual plan
- Paper performance reviews stored in employee HR files

Commitment to Performance Management Process (vertical axis)

Value of Performance Management (horizontal axis)

Exhibit 1-1. Performance Management Maturity Model (adapted from Corporate University Xchange)

ity of HR, and managers may actually get away altogether with not doing appraisals. In these organizations, performance appraisal is not used to link strategy with people, but is merely a paperwork function that has to be done just like expense forms and change orders. We hope this book will help managers in these organizations manage performance and coach, lead, and develop their employees.

Most organizations are in Stage 2 of the PMMM. They have automated the performance appraisal process, it is considered an integral part of every manager's responsibilities, and managers do it with reasonable skill and regularity. It's part of a larger performance management cycle that includes periodic check-ins, coaching, and planning. But it's still not an integral part of overall strategy. When goals are formulated at the highest levels in Stage

2 organizations, there is no concerted effort to drive goals down to the first level of the organization. Strategy may be discussed, PowerPoint presentations may be made, memos may be sent, but the real work of integrating performance appraisals with overall goals is neglected. At the high end of Stage 2, organizations become conscientious about coaching and managing performance and insist that managers adopt a coaching role with their subordinates. Yet despite good intentions, there's little coordinating effort to ensure that coaching and objective writing are done in a consistent and verifiable fashion.

A handful of companies have made it to Stage 3. Not only do they have fully automated performance appraisals in place, but performance management is universally adopted. Tools are readily available in the form of training and coaching, and the organization supports a learning culture from top to bottom. These organizations have learning management processes that are respected and powerful and fully utilized by employees and managers. In the appraisal process, managers in these organizations all use notations directing associates to internal training opportunities and the organization supports and makes readily available improvement efforts.

They train managers in how to conduct performance appraisals, how to coach and counsel, and how to deal with employee problems. They keep records on performance management–related actions by both managers and subordinates and automatically prompt managers when critical events are due. These organizations sometimes describe their HR functions as "talent management" to include succession planning, high-potential programs, mentoring, advanced business training, and careful scrutiny by senior management of people plans throughout the business.

Stage 4 organizations may be as much a theoretical concept as real brick-and-mortar companies. The concept represents a goal to be strived for more than a resting place for companies that have achieved performance appraisal perfection. Stage 4 organizations have all the tools of those at Stage 3 but use them even more dexterously. They have maximized the ability to react to market fluctuations through alignment of people. They plan, execute, and change on a dime. They are masters of continuous improvement without relying on the cumbersome structure of Six Sigma or other organizational overlays. They treat people management and development with the rigor of financial management and can account for the financial impact of training and coaching. They successfully assimilate and orient acquisitions because their culture is both strong and practical and they have a long-term working relationship with customers that surpasses all other partnerships.

The PMMM continuum is dynamic. Once an organization gets to Stage 3 or even 4, the leaders can't rest on their laurels. They must embrace change and accept challenges to their structure. It's a paradox that such cultures are so well integrated that they almost don't need the structure of even the most perfect performance appraisal. But it wasn't always so and it isn't even now. To get to Stages 3 or 4, you need the structures built in Stages 1 and 2.

Regardless of the level at which your organization operates, this book is about helping everyone who aspires to higher levels of communication and performance using tools designed to facilitate that. When performance appraisal is done well, it improves employee motivation, performance, and commitment. It's the goal of this book to help you do that. Doing the things this book recommends won't necessarily get you to Stage 4, but it will help you build a platform of skill that will put you much closer than you may be now.

Performance Management: Six Assumptions

Whatever the situation of performance management in your organization, what you as an individual manager do to manage the performance of your employees is up to you. According to Robert Bacal, author of *Performance Management* (McGraw-Hill, 1999), there are six beliefs or assumptions that are basic to successful performance management:

1. Performance management is a process undertaken with employees and not done to employees.

2. The planning, communicating, and evaluating of performance occur as a partnership (with the exception of "unusual situations that require unilateral disciplinary action").

3. Most employees, once they understand what's expected of them, will make every effort to meet those requirements.

4. The purpose of performance management isn't to look at the past and assign blame but to solve performance problems as they occur and prevent them whenever possible.

5. When performance deficits occur, we need to identify the real causes of the deficit, whether they are causes in the system or causes connected with the individual employee.

6. For the most part, if the manager does his or her job in supporting employees, each employee is really the "resident expert" about the job he or she does and how to improve performance.

Short and Long History

The history of performance appraisal is quite brief.... As a distinct and formal management procedure used in the evaluation of work performance, appraisal really dates from the time of the Second World War—not more than 60 years ago.

Yet in a broader sense, the practice of appraisal is a very ancient art. In the scale of things historical, it might well lay claim to being the world's second oldest profession!

Appraisal, it seems, is both inevitable and universal. In the absence of a carefully structured system of appraisal, people will tend to judge the work performance of others, including subordinates, naturally, informally and arbitrarily.

—Margaret Francis, "Performance Appraisal"

Performance Management Cycle

Many models have been developed for the performance management process, often presented with graphics that may be effective in making some models more appealing, making them seem more correct than other approaches. Keep one point in mind: the best model is one that results in the best performance management results for the specific situation.

In this book we'll use a model for the performance management process, consisting of four stages. This is really a variation on the well-known Plan-Do-Check-Act cycle.

1. **Plan.** Establish expectations for the employee.
2. **Do.** Help the employee perform.
3. **Check.** Appraise the employee's performance.
4. **React.** Act upon the results of the performance appraisal.

Organization of This Book

The chapters of this book won't follow the logic of this performance management cycle. Why not? Because this book is mostly about the performance appraisal process, but that's part of the performance management process, and it's important to remember that. We're going to be occupied mainly with the Plan and Check parts of the process. Managers have expectations and they appraise their employees. Sadly, some may do little or nothing else. After we cover those two phases of the performance management cycle, we then provide some information on Do and React. We consider how you can help your employees perform their jobs better and how you can reinforce your performance appraisals by giving your employees what they deserve.

2 Setting Objectives

G ood objectives link company strategy—the big picture—to what employees do in their jobs and ensure alignment between what employees do and where senior management wants the company to go. When the performance appraisal process is based on objectives, rather than rankings or ratings, it confirms that manager and employee are on the same side, working together.

The objective-setting process can provide a stimulating and creative environment for developing work plans that test and challenge both the employee and the manager to do the best they can and to ensure personal growth and development. The earlier in the performance management cycle you set objectives, the better.

Setting objectives allows you to:

- Create clear performance expectations in advance
- Ensure that employees are working on the right things in the right way
- Focus on measures and results, rather than activities
- Link daily activities to broader business objectives
- Establish a baseline for performance appraisal
- Develop a dialogue with each of your employees on the chal-

lenges and goals of the job

- Initiate discussions of personal and career development

Setting objectives is important, because without good objectives:

- Performance evaluation is subjective and subject to bias
- Employees may remain unclear about job priorities
- New employees may be at a loss as to what to do
- It's difficult to drive strategy into action
- Priorities suffer whenever circumstances change
- Competing priorities can't be evaluated and resourced against overriding goals

In short, without good objectives, the focus of an organization may be lost and employees will be unable to direct their efforts toward those things that ensure the survival and success of the company.

Inspiration from Above

Have you completed your own objective-setting exercise with your manager? If so, how do you feel about the results? What worked well that you'd like to do with your employees? What didn't work so well that you'd like to do better with your employees or not do at all?

The Manager's Role in Setting Objectives

We will assume that you will involve each employee in setting objectives for his or her work. Why? Because it's the smartest way to manage performance. Involvement inspires engagement and commitment, which inspires better performance.

Share the responsibility of setting objectives and benefit from getting input from your employees and showing that you value their collaboration in the performance appraisal process from the start of the cycle.

Set Objectives for Your Work Group

The first step in setting objectives with each of your employees is to set objectives for your work unit. There are basic guidelines that should work in any situation. Objectives may be imposed on you from above, so you may not be completely free to follow the steps below. However, these steps may help you work more effectively with those objectives.

- Understand your company's overall strategy, broad objectives, and vision and how they relate to your team or work group.
- Set objectives for your work unit that are aligned with the organization's objectives.
- Prioritize those objectives.
- Share your objectives with others outside your department—your manager, customers, stakeholders—to get their input.
- Make sure every objective has a distinct measurement standard.
- Meet with all of your employees as a team and review the work unit's objectives. Encourage frank discussion of the objectives and revise them accordingly.
- Give all employees a copy of the unit's objectives and ask them to think about how each of their jobs fits in with the unit's objectives.

The Employee's Role in Setting Objectives

Here's a checklist you can give your employees to help each of them prepare for meeting with you to set individual objectives.

- ❑ Review your performance appraisal and objectives from last year. Indicate for each objective the degree of success you had.
- ❑ If you had difficulty achieving an objective, identify the reasons why that happened. Were there circumstances beyond your control?
- ❑ Consider in what ways your job has changed. What new responsibilities do you have? Do you have clear objectives for those responsibilities? Do you need any additional resources, training, or coaching?
- ❑ Do you have new career aspirations or any personal goals that weren't included in last year's appraisal process but should be included now?

These questions should help your employees think about their evaluations and their responsibilities so they can better prepare for meeting with you to set their objectives. They are necessarily general; you may want to add some more particular questions to this list.

Inputs into the Objective-Setting Process

Here we look at some factors to consider when you and your employees meet to discuss their responsibilities and set objectives. You may make a list of those relevant to your situation, whether for all of your employees or only some of them. Then you might want to give a list to each employee in advance of the meeting or bring the list to the meeting as a guide for your discussion.

Strategic Corporate Goals

Since the primary purpose of performance development is to enable and motivate employees to contribute more effectively and efficiently to the organization, performance objectives should derive from the goals and priorities of the organization. By "goals" we mean outcome statements that define what an organization is trying to accomplish. Goals generally involve major actions and multiple programs, whereas objectives are actions that contribute to attaining goals. (In Chapter 3 we discuss the art of turning goals into objectives.)

Strategic goals are general goals that form part of an organization's corporate strategy. They are targets developed to direct organizational activity. Some strategic goals are easier than others to translate into work unit goals and then into individual performance objectives.

Big-picture corporate goals are often translatable into unit goals when they have as their basis sound metrics. For example, in the heyday of the quality movement, Florida Power and Light had as its chief corporate goal "To become the best managed electric utility in the United States and an excellent company overall and be recognized as such." This inspiring slogan was based on quality metrics, metrics that translated into work unit objectives and performance objectives for employees. Goals like "zero defects" and "zero defections," along with customer satisfaction scores were adopted by work units. However, without those metrics, quality goals, and standards, that strategic goal might have been difficult to translate at the levels of work units and employees.

If your organization uses a balanced scorecard, you can use that to develop performance objectives with your employees.

> **Balanced Scorecard**
> A model consisting of four or five boxes that encompass the top-line metrics of a business, typically the following:
> - Financial metrics
> - Operational or process metrics
> - People or human resource metrics
> - Customer or competitive metrics
> - Metrics associated with learning and growth
>
> The balanced scorecard provides a simple but comprehensive view of the business that helps managers and work units focus on key measures and deliverables that have been determined to drive the success of the enterprise.
>
> The concept was popularized by Robert S. Kaplan and David P. Norton through their book, *The Balanced Scorecard* (Harvard Business School Press, 1996), and articles in *Harvard Business Review*.

Work Unit Objectives

The objectives of the work unit should derive, as noted above, from the organization's strategic goals. In addition, you may want your unit to have other objectives, including objectives that reflect and reinforce the unit's culture. Make sure that your work unit has at least some shared objectives. This will encourage your employees to collaborate and to share resources.

Position Descriptions

Position descriptions are sometimes the most underused sources of objectives. When they are current and detailed, they constitute one of the best sources of objectives a manager can draw on. A good job description describes the responsibilities, tasks, and levels of authority for the position. Often job descriptions have been developed to justify a new position or a position in danger of being eliminated, to establish job requirements for recruiting and hiring, and/or to provide a basis for promoting employees. (In fact, often management provides guidance on promotion by saying, explicitly or implicitly, "When you are doing what employees at the next level are doing, you are ready for promotion.") If position descriptions have been developed carefully and based on research, they can also be a good source of competencies, which in turn can form the basis of many objectives. (We discuss this in Chapter 3.)

However, job descriptions sometimes become so outdated as work responsibilities shift and change that they are of little value in developing performance objectives for the employees in those positions. If you decide to use a job description as input into the objective-setting process, review it carefully and make sure it fits the job. Take notes so you can revise it as necessary later.

Many position descriptions list everything that the employee is expected to do within each functional area. In setting objectives, you should keep the number of objectives for each area reasonable and practical.

Watch out for the Etc.
In many job descriptions, there's a clause that says something like "and other responsibilities as assigned." Such a clause provides necessary flexibility, of course, but it can also allow a job description to be "lazy," to be the equivalent of "Do this and that, *etc.*" Make sure that any "etc. clause" in a job description is not covering significant responsibilities that should be specified.

Think of the job responsibilities in terms of priorities. If you aren't sure how to proceed, here are some guidelines:

- List the areas of responsibilities.
- Rate those responsibilities in order of relative importance in terms of the value of the position to your work unit and the organization. That may be easier if you start by ranking them, beginning with the most important.

- Focus on the essential responsibilities. Maybe all of them seem essential, but if you needed to replace that employee with a temp for a month, you'd probably be able to narrow the list of responsibilities down to the essential ones.

Don't go crazy here with ranking and rating responsibilities. It's probably a good place to apply the Pareto principle. Focus on the "vital few" responsibilities, the 20 percent that constitute 80 percent of the value of the position to your work unit and the organization.

Objectives from Prior Appraisals

One of the best ways to start developing performance objectives is by reviewing performance appraisal documents from the previous year. This provides concrete information on how things went last year and maybe enables you to identify problems with past objectives and with the job descriptions from which those objectives were derived.

Naturally, the value of using objectives from prior appraisals depends on how well those objectives worked and whether the job situation has changed. You may not be able to use prior appraisal documents with all of your employees. If appraisals haven't been satisfactory, maybe the objectives weren't accurate. If that's the case, then you can probably learn from the experience and revise the objectives worth salvaging. However, if the job situation is different, it may be wise for you to take a zero-based approach in setting objectives.

Input from Others

In some situations it may make sense to get input from other people in the workplace. The selection of people who can serve as sources of input for an employee and the relative importance of input from these sources will depend on the nature of the job and the structure and culture of the work unit and the organization.

Results of 360s. 360-degree feedback is a process by which an employee receives confidential feedback anonymously from the people who work around him or her. Typically the employee's manager, peers, and—in the case of managers—direct reports fill out a form that asks questions about a range of work competencies. The employee who is the subject of the 360 may also fill out the form for a self-evaluation.

Organizations typically use a 360-degree feedback process as a performance appraisal tool and/or as a development tool, to help identify development needs through perspectives on the employee's weaknesses and strengths. It can be used to provide input when setting objectives.

> **360-degree feedback** is a process by which an employee receives confidential feedback anonymously from the people who work around him or her. Typically the employee's manager, peers, and—in the case of managers—direct reports fill out a form that asks questions about a range of work competencies. The employee who is the subject of the 360 may also fill out the form for a self-evaluation.

The kinds of objectives that might emerge from 360s are typically related to personal development. They usually address such competencies as communication, organizational skills, teamwork, and other skills that involve the ability of the employee to work with others. They rarely address hard targets like productivity or quality, but their input can be valuable because they can put a numerical target on what might otherwise be a subjective characteristic. They are also powerful in that the results are indisputable: you may disagree with what your peers say, but it's their perception and so it's a fact of life in the workplace.

Since 360s typically focus on subjective impressions, they can ease the pressure on a manager who's trying to communicate deficits in the softer skills like communication, listening, team membership, trust, openness, or attitude. When you get the same feedback from several people who are working around you, you tend to accept it more readily than when it comes from your manager alone.

Comments and Complaints from Customers. Although it makes all the sense in the world to get input from customers when setting performance objectives with employees who have responsibilities that involve contact with customers, this is seldom done directly. Customer input should be considered in setting objectives (and in performance appraisal) only if it can be directly connected to measurable behaviors and results, employee by employee. In call centers, for example, metrics associated with efficiency (answer speed, hold time, resolutions) are often balanced with customer-driven measures such as perceived friendliness, first-call resolution, and tone of voice. It's not always easy to determine the impact of one employee's behavior on overall customer satisfaction, but "double jacking" (when the supervisor listens to customer calls) is a way to directly assess how well an employee is able to connect with customers. It may also be a good idea to solicit input from customers when setting objectives with an employee who works in sales.

Personal Development

I believe that an employee should always have at least one personal development objective that he or she considers a benefit. This objective could provide an opportunity for personal growth, present a challenge, and/or give the employee a chance to prove his or her ability to handle other responsibilities, including those that would come with a promotion. Personal development objectives are good for the employee and good for the manager, in that they motivate employees, which can mean more effective performance management.

Developing Objectives

You and the employee should develop the objectives together, if possible. There are two good ways to do this and one that is not so good.

You can meet with the employee and develop objectives together. Each can prepare for the meeting by jotting down notes about the areas for which you think objectives should be developed and what you think the objective should include.

You can also work on developing objectives together but

apart. You would draft objectives and then give or send them to the employee. He or she would comment on the objectives—the areas covered, the content, the wording, whatever. Objectives should go back and forth until you both feel they're complete.

A way that is not recommended is for you and the employee to develop objectives separately and simultaneously and then try to integrate them. This process would be awkward and it could easily feel adversarial—your objectives vs. the employee's objectives.

Depending on your situation, it may be good to maintain a long-term perspective as you develop objectives. This is smart if you need or want to prepare for changes, whether expected or not, in your work unit and/or the organization. Thinking long-term also provides a context in which to develop objectives for the employee's personal development.

As you develop and discuss the objectives, you should identify any critical issues and possible obstacles. Plan also for resources the employee will need to achieve the objectives.

Finally, it's wise to build flexibility into performance objectives so manager and employee can more easily adapt as changes occur in the job or the work unit. Of course, this is also a good reason to schedule meetings to discuss performance toward those objectives and any issues or difficulties.

Criteria for Effective Objectives

In developing objectives, keep in mind the basic guide for goals expressed in the SMART acronym: Specific, Measurable, Achievable, Relevant, and Time-Bound or Time-Framed.

SMART

We all know about SMART objectives, but we don't all understand the acronym in the same way. There's general agreement on the meaning of S, M, and T. However, A and R are understood in various ways: A may also mean Attainable or Acceptable or even Agreed Upon and R may also mean Realistic or Results-Oriented. (There are several other possibilities for each of the five letters.)

However we understand the meaning of each letter, we should keep in mind the purpose of this acronym: to represent the basic criteria for effective objectives. They should express clearly what you expect from the employee, those expectations should be within his or her power, and they should be expressed in terms that allow you to measure the degree to which the employee has met your expectations.

Specific

- Focus the objective on the results that you expect.
- Use concrete language so that anyone with a basic knowledge of the work area would understand it as you intend.
- Avoid generalities.
- Use action verbs as much as possible, verbs that express behaviors rather than mental processes, attitudes, or feelings.
- Provide details appropriate to the employee's experience and personality. For example, an employee who is very autonomous and/or very experienced will need less detail than an employee with less self-assurance and less experience.

Measurable

- Express the results that you expect in a way that allows for assessing progress and measuring success. When possible, state the results in terms of quantity, quality, cost, and timeliness. Numbers are often good.

Attainable

- Make sure the objective is within the employee's abilities and current skills or skills that he or she could develop within the time frame of the objective.
- Make sure the objective is within the realistic control of the employee. Responsibilities that involve collaboration or cooperation can be problematic in this respect.

Make It Possible
Ensure that the employee has adequate resources to achieve each of the objectives you set, such as time, money, authority, guidance from you, and cooperation from others.

> **Make It Achievable**
> While setting objectives, keep in mind the big picture. You may make sure that each objective is achievable, but if there are too many objectives, the employee may not be able to achieve them all.

*R*elevant
- Ensure that the objective aligns with and supports the objectives of the work unit and the organization.
- Ensure that the employee understands how his or her work toward achieving the objective fits within the greater context of the work unit and the organization.

*R*esults-Oriented
- Specify actual results, not activities.

*T*ime-Bound
- Specify a timeframe. Often the appraisal establishes the timeframe. However, you may want to set interim steps or milestones as a way to monitor progress. Also, some responsibilities are more logically measured by the week, the month, or the quarter.

Meetings to Discuss Progress Toward Objectives

As mentioned earlier, it's a good idea to schedule one-on-one meetings with each of your employees to discuss performance toward their objectives and any issues or potential difficulties. It's not unrealistic to anticipate that job priorities may shift. You can also assume that some objectives may need to be adjusted and that you may need to develop new objectives.

Depending on your situation and the objectives, these meetings could be scheduled quarterly or even monthly. There are at least two advantages in scheduling meetings, rather than meeting when you or the employee feel a need to meet. First, employees are generally unlikely to seek out their boss and say they need to meet—and generally feel uncomfortable when their boss suggests there's a need for a meeting. Second, meetings are more likely to happen if they're scheduled than if they're left up to either manager or employee to suggest.

SMARTER Than SMART

You can go beyond the SMART guidelines. There's also SMARTER, which adds "ethical" or "encompassing" or "exciting" and "recorded" or "rewarding" (and other possibilities). Some proponents of SMARTER have developed SMARTER2–Specific, Measurable, Agreed, Realistic, Time-Bound, Evaluated, and Reviewed *and* Strategic, Meaningful, Attainable, Rewarding, Team-Building, Empowering, and Rewarding. Whew!

These and the various other SMART/SMARTER criteria are probably all more or less good to keep in mind when setting objectives. However, it seems that a good objective should answer three basic questions for the employee:

- What do you expect me to do?
- By when?
- How will I know whether I've done it right?

SMART objectives help reduce subjectivity, ensure that manager and employee have the same set of expectations, and understand them in the same way.

If you're unsure about how to word performance objectives, you might benefit from consulting *Perfect Phrases for Setting Performance Goals,* (2nd Edition) by Robert Bacal (McGraw-Hill, 2011). However, although the subtitle promises "Hundreds of Ready-to-Use Goals," I advise you to consider these only for inspiration and guidance.

This chapter has been all about maximizing the benefits of being free to conduct performance appraisals in whatever way you feel would be most effective for performance management and most appropriate for your employees and the culture of your work unit and the organization. In the next chapter, the second part of the Plan stage in the Plan-Do-Check-React cycle of performance management, we consider the possibilities if you have little or no freedom in your performance appraisals.

3 Improving on Performance Appraisal Forms

All performance appraisal forms are different, yet all performance appraisal forms are the same. All require the manager to evaluate his or her employees against some standards or criteria—objectives, competencies, and goals.

Louis Sullivan, the great American architect whose name is associated with the steel-and-glass skyscraper, famously stated, "Form follows function." (Actually, he wrote, "Form *ever* follows function," but why quibble?) What he meant was that things should be made in a way that suits their intended purpose and use.

Unfortunately, this is not always the case with performance appraisal forms. The array of performance appraisal forms in use today more closely resembles the Tower of Babel than a sleek skyscraper. Every company has its own form and, while they all have many things in common (sections for objectives, something on traits or competencies, open boxes for written comments), they are all a little different—and most leave managers struggling with definitions, limited discretion, new terminology, and lots of room for flowery prose. The human resource department, which typically owns the forms and the performance appraisal process, requires that managers, who are most comfortable with checklists and lots of structure, become talented writers able to sum up the skills, abilities, and potential of each of their employees in 250 words or less.

If this is your situation and there is only one form available to you, you can struggle with that form or you can take responsibility for using it to its best advantage. You can do things to make the form follow function at least a little better. This chapter provides guidance for working with some of the standard sections you are likely to find on your form.

Completing the Objectives Section

Nearly all performance appraisal forms have an objectives section. Sometimes they are completely blank, numbered objective 1, 2, 3, and so forth, and sometimes they have space for dates, percentage of total, timing, and whatnot.

Using the 4Ws and 1H to Turn Goals into Objectives

Before you even touch the form, write out the objectives, starting from the goals of the organization and the work unit. By "goals" we mean outcome statements that define what an organization or a work unit is trying to accomplish. Goals generally involve major actions and multiple programs. An example of a goal might be to grow income by 15 percent. In contrast, by "objectives" we mean here actions that contribute to attaining a goal. Objectives typically must be related directly to the goal; they must be stated in terms of results that are measurable and have a timeframe for completion; and they must be precise, clear, concise, and understandable.

Writing objectives will always be something of an art form, but there are things you can do to put a hard edge on the overall good intentions of complex goals.

I advise using the method of 4Ws and 1H. This stands for Who, What, When, Why, and How Much. Do this even before you try to make your objectives SMART.

Any objective can be structured using the 4Ws and 1H method.

Let's take a set of goals and sharpen them up into a useful objective using the 4Ws and 1H technique.

> Call center employees have experienced frustration in trying to use the online help desk to get quick answers to customer inquiries. The current system is slow and sometimes takes as long as 5 minutes to provide an answer while the customer is on hold. Employees are resistant to using it and less than 40 percent do so currently. We must double this. We need to improve the system so that turnaround time is faster and responses more accurate. At the same time, we want to make sure employees are comfortable with the system and fully use it. These changes need to be in place by the end of the first quarter and provide stable and consistent results before year end.

Wow, that's a mouthful. But it's only one goal, with the seeds of a good crisp objective buried within. Here's how that objective might read after being put through the 4Ws and 1H process.

> The electronic help desk will be up and running during the first quarter of this year and in use by over 85 percent of employees. Time to locate answers to commonly asked questions will decrease by 25 percent with at least 95 percent accuracy within the first half of the year and satisfaction by employees using the system will achieve a rating of at least 75 percent favorability before year end.

Who: Technical help desk team. Internal and external customers.

What: Improve electronic Help Desk Effectiveness and Efficiency.

When: First quarter and year-end.

Why: Increased efficiency and satisfaction.

How Much: Availability, utilization, time to answer, accuracy, and employee satisfaction.

Objective writing will always be something of an art form, but by using the 4Ws and 1H, you can put a hard edge to the overall good intentions of complex goals. Use the following worksheet to turn your goals into objectives.

4Ws and 1H	What They Mean	Your Objective
Who	Name the individuals involved including who's responsible for achieving the objectives and those who will be affected. Identify stakeholders and customers as well.	
What	What specifically is the task that this objective focuses on?	
When	What are the critical dates when deliverables are due?	
Why	What are the outcomes or results that will come from this objective?	
How Much	What are the measures or metrics that will be tracked in connection to this objective?	

Turning Competencies into Objectives

As a manager, you may be asked to use a set of competencies to evaluate performance and set objectives. That is all well and good, but competencies are not objectives and unless they are SMART, they may be too subjective to provide good measures of behavior.

Competencies are identified behaviors, knowledge, skills, and abilities that directly contribute to the success of employees and the organization. The purpose of a competency is to describe desired behaviors through the use of performance indicators or measures that fit under a specific category. Competencies should be anchored in research that validates them against the job in question and they should have measurable behavioral statements associated with them.

Competency A competency is an identified behavior, knowledge, skill, or ability that directly contributes to the success of employees and the organization. The purpose of a competency is to describe desired behaviors through the use of performance indicators or measures that fit under a specific category.

The example below for the competency Collaboration and Teamwork begins with a definition and then provides examples of how that competency can be observed and measured in the workplace through performance indicators.

Collaboration and Teamwork

Supports a positive team environment in which members participate, respect, and cooperate with each other to achieve desired results.

Examples of performance indicators:
- Collaborates with others to improve quality and address needs
- Builds and sustains cooperative working relationships
- Contributes to the resolution of workplace conflict
- Demonstrates a sense of responsibility for the success of the group or department
- Demonstrates a positive attitude in work assignment and interaction with others
- Recognizes strengths and contributions of others
- Provides leadership on projects and/or programs

When performance objectives are based on behaviors that are not readily quantifiable, using competencies can provide a framework for both evaluation and goal setting while the performance indicators show the way to improve performance through examples.

You may be asked to use a set of competencies to evaluate performance. However, competencies are not objectives and, unless they are SMART, they may be too subjective to provide good measures of behavior.

Let's take our example of the competency of collaboration and teamwork along with examples of performance indicators. The examples are a good first step, but performance indicators aren't good objectives either. To be effective objectives, examples must be written in such a way that the competency can be observed, measured, and evaluated.

Here is how this competency of collaboration and teamwork might be turned into some objectives.

Objectives

1. Leads a process improvement team through the entire prob-

lem-solving cycle, achieving reduction in defects while maintaining team member satisfaction of 90 percent favorable.

2. Achieves average score of 4 or better on all customer satisfaction ratings.
3. Receives positive feedback on 360° assessments from all stakeholders.
4. Increases referrals from clients by 25 percent of consulting assignments.

Using Action Verbs

Writing objectives involves translating good intentions into hard measures. Benjamin S. Bloom, an educational psychologist, created a classification of educational objectives for the cognitive domain that we can use in writing performance objectives. Exhibit 3-1 shows how lower levels of cognitive engagement (knowledge, comprehension) differ from higher levels (analysis, synthesis, and evaluation). It also shows how action verbs can trigger objectives at those levels of engagement.

As mentioned earlier, one of the key elements to writing a good objective is to use action verbs. Here's a short of list of verbs that should serve as a useful guide to preparing good objectives.

• Classify	• Diagram	• Name
• Compose	• Distinguish	• Order
• Construct	• Estimate	• Reduce
• Decode	• Evaluate	• Remove
• Define	• Label	• Reengineer
• Demonstrate	• List	• Reproduce
• Describe	• Locate	• Sell
• Identify	• Make	• Solve
• Interpret	• Measure	• Translate

In developing objectives from competencies, remember to use the SMART criteria discussed earlier. Make sure your objectives are *S*pecific, *M*easurable, *A*ttainable, *R*elevant and *R*esults-oriented, and *T*ime-bound.

	Engagement Levels	Verbs Used for Objectives
Lowest Level	Knowledge	define, memorize, repeat, record, list, recall, name, relate, collect, label, specify, cite, enumerate, tell, recount
	Comprehension	restate, summarize, discuss, describe, recognize, explain, express, identify, locate, report, retell, review, translate
	Application	exhibit, solve, interview, simulate, apply, employ, use, demonstrate, dramatize, practice, illustrate, operate, calculate, show, experiment
	Analysis	interpret, classify, analyze, arrange, differentiate, group, compare, organize, contrast, examine, scrutinize, survey, categorize, dissect, probe, inventory, investigate, question, discover, inquire, distinguish, detect, diagram, inspect
	Synthesis	compose, set up, plan, prepare, propose, imagine, produce, hypothesize, invent, incorporate, develop, generalize, design, originate, formulate, predict, arrange, contrive, assemble, concoct, construct, systematize, create
Highest Level	Evaluation	judge, assess, decide, measure, appraise, estimate, evaluate, infer, rate, deduce, compare, score, value, predict, revise, choose, conclude, recommend, select, determine, criticize

Exhibit 3-1. Verbs for Different Levels of Cognitive Engagement (adapted from Benjamin S. Bloom, *Taxonomy of Educational Objectives, Handbook I: The Cognitive Domain*, Addison-Wesley, 1956)

Working with Final Ratings

With very few exceptions, the final outcome of a performance evaluation is a number. There have always been objections to reducing a year's worth of work to a single number, but in the end, most organizations want to have something specific that can be used to make decisions about pay, promotions, training and development, and so forth.

Most forms use a five-point scale with labels such as *Greatly Exceeds Expectations*, *Exceeds Expectations*, *Meets Expectations*, *Occasionally Meets Expectations*, and *Unsatisfactory.* Sometimes this final score is an average: each competency or objective is rated, the scores are added, and the sum is divided by the number of ratings.

Behaviorally Anchored Rating Scale

A more objective way to arrive at numerical ratings is through the use of a *behaviorally anchored rating scale.* These can help the manager by providing examples of what performance would merit a rating of "3," for example.

> **Behaviorally anchored rating scales (BARS)** are rating scales with scale points defined by statements of effective and ineffective behaviors. BARS differ from other rating scales in that scale points are behaviors defined specifically.

Behaviorally anchored rating scales (BARS) are rating scales with scale points defined by statements of effective and ineffective behaviors. BARS differ from other rating scales in that scale points are behaviors defined specifically.

Exhibit 3-2 shows an example of how a competency is broken down into performance indicators, each of which becomes a subcompetency and gets a behaviorally anchored rating. Subjective decisions based on observation and supplementary data don't get much more objective than this.

If your organization's performance appraisal form does not provide behaviorally anchored rating scales, you can develop your way of thinking in terms of behaviors based on what you observe. High ratings should have specific deliverables that quantify into important measures such as cost, time, or quality. Midpoint ratings should be characterized by good efforts, such as "developed," "produced," "improved," and other terms that address improvement of knowledge and awareness rather than hard outcomes. Lower ratings, of course, should show a failure to

Communication: Clearly conveys and receives information and ideas through a variety of media to individuals or groups in a manner that engages the listeners, helps them understand and retain the message, and invites response and feedback. Keeps others informed as appropriate. Demonstrates good written, oral, and listening skills.

Ratings Performance Indicators	Greatly Exceeds Expectations 5	Exceeds Expectations 4	Meets Expectations 3	Needs Development 2	Unsatisfactory 1
Organization and Clarity	Conveys thoughts and ideas so as to avoid misunderstandings. Communicates with needs and expectations of audience in mind.		Conveys thoughts clearly and concisely.		Has difficulty expressing thoughts.
Listening Skills	Listens with demonstrated understanding and empathy. Thoughtfully explores topic as appropriate.		Listens actively and attentively and asks appropriate questions.		Fails to listen and share feedback.
Keeping Others Informed	Continuously fulfills all knowledge requirements of supervisors, co-workers, and others.		Keeps supervisors, coworkers, and others well informed.		Fails to share important information or passes on trivia.

Exhibit 3-2. Competency, Performance Indicators, and Ratings

Ratings Performance Indicators	Greatly Exceeds Expectations 5	Exceeds Expectations 4	Meets Expectations 3	Needs Development 2	Unsatisfactory 1
Written Communication	Communications are error-free, have positive tone, and seem professionally written.		Communicates well in writing.		Written communications are unclear and disorganized, lack substance, and contain grammatical and/or spelling errors.
Sensitivity to Others	Continuously tailors communications to match the listeners; uses appropriate style, level of detail, grammar, and organization of thoughts to actively engage the listeners.		Consistently sensitive to cultural, gender, educational, and other individual characteristics when communicating with others.		Insensitive to cultural, gender, educational, and other individual characteristics when communicating with others.
Comments					

Exhibit 3-2. (Continued)

perform in either attitudes or outcomes. (Descriptions that include terms such as "awareness" and "attitudes" are not actually behaviorally anchored, of course, because awareness and attitudes are not observable behaviors.)

Between "Always" and "Never"
Avoid using vague quantifying adverbs in your behaviorally anchored rating scales. We could probably all agree that "always" means 100 percent of the time and "never" means 0 percent of the time. But how much agreement would there be on adverbs such as "sometimes" and "usually" and "occasionally"?

Competencies with Descriptors and Behavioral Indicators

Exhibit 3-3 on pages 32–39 presents examples of frequently used competencies with descriptions and behavioral indicators.

Another Dimension of Performance–Potential

Many appraisal forms ask for determinations of both performance and potential. It is generally difficult or impossible to determine potential, unless through aptitude and intelligence tests.

However, using determinations of both performance and potential allows for better decisions on which employees would benefit from development resources such as training and coaching.

For example, two employees are both appraised as outstanding performers. However, one is determined to have no more potential than necessary to do his current job and the other is determined to have great potential. The latter could benefit from development resources but not the former. The manager can invest more wisely in developing his or her employees when potential is assessed in addition to performance. Later in this book we will discuss career coaching and how considerations of both performance and potential play a role in developing employees.

Performance and Potential: Options for Coaching and Development

If you are assessing potential as well as performance and you are using a simple rating scale for each, you could try this idea for combining the two.

Competency	ADAPTABILITY
Description	Demonstrates the willingness and ability to adapt to changing situations
Behavioral Indicators	• Accepts and adapts to internal or external change or redirection • Demonstrates flexibility and resilience in the face of uncertainty or ambiguity • Learns new tasks or information with ease and without frustration • Works effectively within a fast-paced, evolving environment
Competency	COACHING
Description	Helps others increase their capabilities and maximize their potential through individualized development support
Behavioral Indicators	• Assists in the development of job skills in a planned, systematic way • Explains concepts and procedures clearly, adapting coaching technique to learning style of associates • Models intended behavior • Provides timely, constructive, and behaviorally specific feedback • Acknowledges and reinforces strengths of individuals
Competency	COMMITMENT AND CREDIBILITY
Description	Projects commitment, credibility, and reliability, inspiring confidence and trust
Behavioral Indicators	• Is honest and forthright • Responds to challenging situations with a positive, can-do attitude • Takes responsibility for own actions • Keeps commitments • Displays commitment to excellence through self-imposed high standards • Exhibits tenacity and persistence in achieving a goal • Remains calm and productive in stressful situations

Exhibit 3-3. Frequently Used Competencies with Descriptions and Behavioral Indicators (Continued on pages 33–39)

Competency	COMMUNICATION SKILLS
Description	Conveys information in a way that brings about understanding
Behavioral Indicators	• Articulates ideas and conveys information effectively in both individual and group situations • Practices active listening by looking for verbal and nonverbal cues, seeking clarification, and checking for understanding • Asks probing questions to gain a better understanding of underlying concerns or issues • Writes clearly and concisely, using proper grammar and business writing techniques • Adapts communication method, style, and content to the audience and the situation
Competency	INFLUENCE
Description	Persuades others to accept a point of view or follow a course of action
Behavioral Indicators	• Identifies decision makers and targets influence efforts toward them • Involves all affected parties in a process or decision to ensure their support • Creates strong, logical arguments and cites several reasons to support the desired course of action • Employs consensus-building skills to achieve win–win outcomes
Competency	INNOVATION
Description	Generates new ideas and innovative solutions
Behavioral Indicators	• Thinks "outside the boundaries" or apparent limitations of a situation • Looks at situations or problems from different angles • Sees possibilities that others have not noticed • Generates imaginative, forward-looking ideas or solutions • Finds ways of improving what is already effective
Competency	INTERPERSONAL RELATIONSHIPS
Description	Develops strong, positive interpersonal relationships with colleagues and customers
Behavioral Indicators	• Relates well with people regardless of their personality characteristics, level of expertise, or position within the organization • Consistently treats others with dignity and respect • Accepts others and acknowledges their perspectives, feelings, and ideas • Recognizes and responds to cues that suggest underlying reasons or motives for people's behavior

Exhibit 3-3. (Continued)

Competency	PRESENTATION SKILLS
Description	Delivers high-impact, credible, and informative presentations
Behavioral Indicators	• Creates well-organized presentations that build a clear, compelling story or logical sequence of ideas • Tailors content and style to the level and understanding of the audience • Engages the audience and holds their attention using a variety of techniques • Uses visuals effectively to enhance the impact and clarity of the message • Responds and adapts to audience needs and concerns
Competency	TEAMWORK AND COLLABORATION
Description	Works cooperatively and collaboratively with teams and business partners to achieve goals
Behavioral Indicators	• Proactively shares information, expertise, and experience with other team members • Solicits input from others and gives credit to contributors • Develops collaborative working relationships across groups and functions • Backs up team members and offers support to peers and others who need it
Competency	WORKLOAD MANAGEMENT
Description	Demonstrates a focused, organized, and systematic approach to accomplishing tasks and achieving goals
Behavioral Indicators	• Effectively prioritizes workload based on urgency, importance, and client expectations • Demonstrates strong organization and time management skills • Manages multiple tasks or projects simultaneously without losing focus or sacrificing quality • Identifies opportunities for process improvements and implements them, leveraging appropriate and available resources and tools
Competency	CALL HANDLING SKILLS
Description	Demonstrates service excellence over the phone, providing suitable information and using the appropriate channels and guidelines
Behavioral Indicators	• Establishes and maintains rapport with customers, making them feel unique and valued • Probes to uncover both stated and unstated needs • Maintains control and directs the flow of the call • Consistently follows call handling protocols, models, and guidelines

Exhibit 3-3. (Continued)

Competency	BUSINESS ACUMEN
Description	Applies business knowledge and experience to all decisions and actions
Behavioral Indicators	• Demonstrates understanding of the relative business/financial impact of specific decisions on the organization • Understands how decisions or actions at one level affect different parts of the organization • Demonstrates a broad-based understanding of risk management and takes measures to minimize/manage risk • Uses sound judgment in balancing customer requests with potential risk and organizational goals
Competency	CHANGE MANAGEMENT
Description	Champions and facilitates change through appropriate planning and communication
Behavioral Indicators	• Describes and positions upcoming change within the context of business needs • Proactively communicates the details about what is changing and what is not • Anticipates and plans for the impact of change on individuals and the organization • Encourages open communication and deals constructively with rumors and resistance
Competency	CLIENT CONSULTING
Description	Focuses on understanding and responding to client needs
Behavioral Indicators	• Assumes a consultative role to acquire a clear understanding of the business need and the client's perception of relevant issues • Probes to uncover underlying issues or unspoken concerns • Influences and supports the client in accepting new processes, products, and technologies • Identifies the client's scope of influence, decision-making authority, and key stakeholders within his/her organization • Ensures client satisfaction by seeking feedback and providing follow-up on client requests

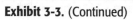

Exhibit 3-3. (Continued)

Competency	RELATIONSHIP MANAGEMENT
Description	Develops, manages, and maintains strong client relationships
Behavioral Indicators	• Builds strong partnerships based on shared commitment to mutual goals • Establishes and meets client expectations throughout the course of the relationship • Demonstrates ultimate ownership and accountability for client relationships • Keeps clients' interests in mind and acts as their advocate with internal groups • Educates the client about their role and expectations of them during the project (e.g., responsibilities, resources needed, deadlines)
Competency	CUSTOMER BUSINESS KNOWLEDGE
Description	Interacts with clients with an understanding of their business: their organizational structure, their business plans, and their goals
Behavioral Indicators	• In interactions with clients is sensitive to their culture: their people, norms, and "hot buttons" • Identifies how the company's products and services impact the clients' business plans and goals • Acknowledges client preferences regarding which people to contact for which kinds of information or issues • Identifies how decisions are made in the clients' organizations and who makes them • Researches the past, current, and potential future relationships of clients with the company and factors that information into client interactions and action plans
Competency	ORGANIZATIONAL AWARENESS
Description	Knows how the organization works and how to work effectively within it
Behavioral Indicators	• Demonstrates knowledge of the organizational structure of the company and its various parts • Demonstrates knowledge of the company's business goals and the associates' roles in achieving them • Adheres to processes, procedures, and standards of the organization • Finds and uses resources across the organization that can provide assistance in accomplishing work • Considers how actions and decisions affect different parts of the organization • Respects the procedures, priorities, and constraints of groups with which he or she interacts

Exhibit 3-3. (Continued)

Competency	PROBLEM RESOLUTION
Description	Anticipates, analyzes, and effectively resolves problems and issues
Behavioral Indicators	• Takes personal responsibility for solving a problem or finding a resource that can help do so • Identifies when and how to escalate problems to the appropriate level • Seeks out data and information to identify underlying causes of the problem • Provides timely resolution and follow-through • Sets realistic expectations and timeframes for resolution • Generates new ideas, innovative solutions, and viable alternatives to resolve problems
Competency	PROCESS IMPROVEMENT
Description	Analyzes processes and identifies areas for improvement
Behavioral Indicators	• Identifies the elements of a process, including the process flow, potential trouble spots, and dependencies on other groups • Monitors processes continuously by looking at trends in output quality, efficiency (cost, time, resources), and trouble spots • Institutes or uses valid and reliable quality measures • Considers existing best practices while seeking opportunities for improvement • Designs and recommends process improvements that can reduce or eliminate problems and increase quality and efficiency
Competency	PRODUCT AND SERVICE KNOWLEDGE
Description	Demonstrates a working knowledge of products and services as they apply to his or her job
Behavioral Indicators	• Uses available resources to quickly find product and service information • Describes features and benefits of products and services, including technical and legal requirements, and related services • Describes how the product or service will work in the customer's environment

Exhibit 3-3. (Continued)

Competency	PROJECT MANAGEMENT
Description	Establishes a clearly defined course of action to organize work and achieve goals
Behavioral Indicators	• Accurately scopes projects and develops realistic, workable plans and timelines • Identifies and delegates tasks, with concrete schedules and criteria for successful completion • Effectively manages project incorporating appropriate communication, feedback, and follow-through • Proactively monitors progress, addressing issues and making mid-course adjustments as needed • Ensures the appropriate level of stakeholder involvement
Competency	RESEARCH AND ANALYSIS
Description	Gathers relevant information, identifies relationships, reasons from cause to effect, and draws logical conclusions
Behavioral Indicators	• Seeks information from multiple sources • Separates critical from noncritical information • Synthesizes complex and diverse information to identify trends and relationships that may influence conclusions • Draws logical conclusions based on examination and evaluation of data • Presents conclusions and recommendations clearly
Competency	RISK MANAGEMENT
Description	Balances the potential risk with the potential for gain in financial, reputational, operational, and strategic decisions
Behavioral Indicators	• Identifies potential risks in daily activities, communicates, and escalates appropriately • Keeps abreast of and uses effective contingency plans • Consistently adheres to applicable compliance, legal, and regulatory rules and guidelines • Weighs costs and benefits as they relate to risk control • Proactively works to protect the firm from legal, financial, and reputation exposure

Exhibit 3-3. (Continued)

Competency	TECHNOLOGY SKILLS
Description	Utilizes systems and tools effectively and efficiently to accomplish work
Behavioral Indicators	• Demonstrates general computer literacy • Demonstrates a working knowledge of the functionality and interdependencies of systems and technologies related to his/her own job responsibilities • Navigates the intranet and the Internet to collect information and research issues • Quickly learns and applies new technology developments and enhancements as they relate to his/her job
Competency	TRANSACTION PROCESSING
Description	Demonstrates a mastery of transaction processing and understands how individual transactions impact the delivery of products and services
Behavioral Indicators	• Accurately and efficiently processes transactions, using multiple operating platforms • Adheres to all applicable procedures and regulatory requirements • Demonstrates an understanding of how the tasks and transactions performed by various functional groups fit within the larger operational context • Identifies the impact of transaction errors on cost, customer satisfaction, and compliance

Exhibit 3-3. (Continued)

One company used color codes for the four-point scale it used to rate performance and potential separately:

- Red for poor performance or for little or no potential
- Yellow for problematic performance or for low or untapped potential
- Green for good performance or for good potential
- Blue for outstanding performance or for great potential

The company combined the ratings to produce 16 possible ratings (Exhibit 3-4).

With this use of potential and performance combinations, a new set of possibilities emerged. It opened options for coaching

Potential / Performance	Blue	Green	Yellow	Red
Blue	Excellent performance, promote short term	Excellent performance, promote within six months	Excellent performance, consider increased responsibilities	Outstanding, but likely to remain in current job
Green	In good standing in current job	Good performance/ Enhance coaching	Good performance, begin to seek other opportunities	Good performance, broaden scope of responsibility immediately
Yellow	Performance plan	Performance improving/ maintain vigilance	Average performance, consider enhanced career development training	Focus on performance improvement and coaching immediately
Red	Immediate outplacement	Performance plan	Discuss career aspiration and consider fit in present job	Make an effort to redesign job or find another job with better fit

Exhibit 3-4. Performance and Potential: Options for Coaching and Development

and development. An employee who is an outstanding performer but has limited potential might be considered to be placed correctly in his or her current job. An employee with super-high potential could be performing poorly due to a bad job placement or other factor. Later in this book we will discuss career coaching and how considerations of both performance and potential play a role in developing employees.

Technology and Performance Appraisals

Many companies use computer-based forms and are doing more than just adding word processing to the performance appraisal process. The great advantage of computer-based forms is that they enable manager and employee to collaborate more easily on developing objectives as well as gathering input from significant stakeholders.

Computers facilitate the process—and make it easier for you to type away and immediately e-mail your first thoughts throughout the known universe. Before you commit anything to electrons, do your homework. Get input from others. Write out the objectives using the 4Ws and 1H or SMART techniques. The growing habit of shooting off unedited e-mails should not be allowed to influence the serious business of writing objectives.

The best computer-based appraisal software can provide information on past performance and key events during the year, to queue up new objectives, and allow the manager to see last year's appraisal side by side with this year's. It can also present metric information from dashboards with current data bearing on performance goals. This is fairly sophisticated and requires extensive data gathering and electronic monitoring systems, but it's the wave of the future.

Don't Get Lazy with Technology

The technology that also enables managers to keep performance appraisals in their computers or company networks online unfortunately enables the lazy and unscrupulous to just change the dates year after year. Saving time and energy has a downside in performance management: employees who work harder and smarter but get the same evaluation as the year before may not feel so motivated to work harder and smarter again.

Here's some advice to consider in using electronic systems.

- Don't be constrained by the system. If it doesn't allow the flexibility you need to develop your objectives, don't use it until final documentation.
- Use Microsoft Word for first-pass development. Most systems allow for editing, but not as well as Word, which tracks changes and provides a history.
- Don't keep the document virtual. Print it out and review it with the employee. Keep it in a file the old-fashioned way. This makes it more real and the employee is more likely to read it.
- Don't send your performance appraisal documents via smartphone. It trivializes the appraisal process and makes the documents hard to read.

While electronic systems make documentation and record keeping easier, there is no substitute for the human touch. Don't allow the system to replace personal contact and discussion.

At this point we leave the Plan stage of the Plan, Do, Check, React performance management cycle and move into the Check stage.

4 | Evaluating Your Employees

Now you've got your evaluation forms and all your documentation and notes and so on. Now it's time to evaluate your employees.

Whether you've got one employee or one hundred, treat each as an individual. Allow enough time for each evaluation and focus appropriately on each employee as if he or she were your only one. This is what we do here: focus on how you should prepare for each of your employees.

Actually, you should start the preparation about a month in advance of scheduling appraisal meetings. Meet with all of your employees as a group and explain the purpose for the performance appraisals and how you and they will do their appraisals. Tell them what's going to happen before they meet with you individually and what's going to happen during the meeting. Encourage them at that time to ask questions, either then or in the coming weeks.

Words of Wisdom

"One of the most common mistakes managers make is to conduct a performance evaluation without being fully prepared. Employees quickly realize when a supervisor has not taken adequate time to prepare their annual review.

"Although it is the one time a manager can truly emphasize the value an employee adds to his or her team, too often the opportunity is never recognized or taken full advantage of.

"It's an opportunity that is simply lost—for both parties.

"Managers who have not adequately prepared are quickly seen by their employees as being uncaring and self-centered."

—Richard Gorham, *www.leadership-tools.com*

Schedule the Meeting and Prepare Your Employee

Schedule the meeting for a time convenient for both of you. Allow the employee enough time to prepare for the meeting. Generally, a week should be sufficient to prepare, including a self-evaluation. Some experts suggest allowing two weeks. You know your employees, their workloads, and their work habits, so you should decide accordingly. Many employees—like many managers—may procrastinate and worry, so more time is not better.

Schedule at least an hour. It's important to allow time for the employee to react to the evaluation, to discuss it and ask questions, and to bring up issues.

I remember reading somewhere a recommendation to schedule as much as four hours. I don't agree. If you've been communicating with your employees regularly during the evaluation period about how they've been doing their jobs, you don't need much time to discuss their performance at the end of the period. If a performance appraisal meeting lasts more than an hour or two, it's likely for one or more of the following reasons:

- The manager has not planned appropriately.
- The manager has not given the employee enough guidance to prepare.
- The employee has not planned sufficiently.
- The discussion has gone off track and/or become emotional.

- The meeting entered into planning for the next evaluation period.

Whatever the reason for the meeting to run long, it's generally advisable to try to end it at the scheduled time. After all, how much meeting can manager and employee endure? If necessary, you can meet again and finish the evaluation process.

You should choose a location for the meeting that will allow you and the employee to work in quiet and privacy, without interruptions, and in comfort. Ensuring the proper setting and atmosphere for your meeting not only is smart in terms of productivity, but also shows respect for your employee.

Give your employee an idea of what to expect and how to prepare for the meeting. Give him or her a copy of the performance appraisal process and the evaluation form you're using or a self-evaluation form, if you intend to elicit written input. This is generally a good idea: it makes the performance appraisal process more collaborative. Even if you don't intend to elicit written input, asking your employee to do a self-evaluation is a way to engage him or her in a valuable experience, since it compels the employee to go through the evaluation from your perspective and better prepares him or her for the discussion.

Whether you choose to have your employees do a self-evaluation or not, I'd suggest providing them with some questions like the following to help them prepare for the appraisal meeting:

- What are your primary job duties and responsibilities?
- How would you rate your past year on the job—good, satisfactory, unsatisfactory, or bad? Why?
- What would you consider to be your three most important achievements this past year?
- What aspects of your job do you find most difficult?
- What aspects of your job do you find most satisfying?
- What aspects of your job interest you the most?
- What aspects of your job interest you the least?

"The review process is a partnership," Robert Bacal stresses in his book, *Performance Management* (McGraw-Hill, 1999, p. 113). "It's a problem-solving process." That's why you should ask them to evaluate themselves. "They are in the best position to figure out how they can do their jobs better." Performance appraisals are "about looking forward, not looking backward."

Make sure that your employee has an accurate and detailed job description, so he or she knows the basis for your evaluation. If there is no such description, maybe the two of you should first meet to draft one.

The more you can help your employee prepare for the meeting, the easier and more productive the meeting can be for both of you. Nobody can guarantee that it will be fun, but if you can minimize the stress and maximize the benefits of the discussion, it's effort well invested.

A day or two before your scheduled meeting with the employee, send him or her a short memo or e-mail that summarizes the performance appraisal process, as a reminder of the meeting and of the explanation you provided weeks earlier.

Be Serious About Scheduling

Take scheduled appraisal meetings seriously. "Managers often bump scheduled appraisal meetings when other, 'more important' things come up," Robert Bacal notes in his book, *Performance Management* (McGraw-Hill, 1999). "Bad idea. This sends the message that you're not serious about the process, that it's not a high priority. Schedule it and stick to the schedule."

Decide on Your Approach

Why are you doing performance appraisals? What are your goals? You want to improve your employees' performance, of course. You want to discuss any difficulties. You probably want to reward good performance and deal with problematic performance. Do you also want to establish new performance expectations? Do you have any other goals? Keep your goals and priorities in mind as you proceed through this phase of the performance appraisal process.

Evaluate Your Employee

You may already have at hand and organized all the materials you'll need to evaluate your employee—or the pieces of the puzzle may be scattered about, on your computer, in your file cabinet, on your shelves.... The materials will include some or all of the following:

- Job description
- Performance plan or list of performance objectives (with measures and time frames)
- Records of accomplishments
- Notes from any conversations during the evaluation period about his or her performance
- Comments on his or her performance from other sources (e.g., coworkers, employees in other work units, other managers, customers or clients)

As you review the employee's job description, make a note of revisions you should make—new responsibilities, changes in focus and priorities, responsibilities no longer part of the job, and so on—and questions you want to ask the employee. (Job descriptions often stay the same as the job situation changes and a manager may not always be aware of all the changes in his or her employees' responsibilities.)

Begin with the Best

When you begin to do the evaluations, it's generally smartest to begin with your best employees. There are at least three good reasons for doing so:

1. It's generally easier to evaluate better employees.
2. If the employees are easier to evaluate, you can become more comfortable with the evaluation forms and work more efficiently through the process.
3. By starting with your best employees, you develop a more real sense of what you should be able to expect from your employees—and you should become aware of general issues

in your workplace that may negatively affect how your employees do their jobs.

Do evaluations for only two or three of your best employees. Then, if you can group your employees by tasks and/or responsibilities, it would probably be logical and easier to do the evaluations by group. If not, do them without any order.

It may seem more efficient to continue doing evaluations from your better employees and working your way down through the others, but that would mean you'd be dealing with the more difficult employees when you're feeling most tired of doing evaluations and probably dreading the final ones, so you'd probably be evaluating more harshly. That would be bad for those employees and bad for you.

Review the Evaluation Period

With each employee, it's smart to start by mentally reviewing the evaluation period and jotting notes about his or her performance and behavior. Record anything that comes to mind, just letting memories and thoughts flow. Then, when you've jotted down everything that you remember and are feeling focused on the employee, you can do the evaluation more efficiently and probably more accurately.

Also, if you are providing a narrative for each evaluation item and rating or for sections of the form, you should have in the notes from your "brain dump" enough to write about the employee without straining your brain.

Next, review your employee's performance plan, if any. What was expected of him or her for the past evaluation period? Assess his or her performance against the standards in the performance plan.

Also review any file of achievements and accomplishments for that employee (e.g., important deadlines met, special projects completed, significant problems solved, etc.).

After you've completed your review of the employee, it's time to move on to rating.

Rate the Performance

You don't need instructions here. You have your evaluation forms, as discussed in Chapters 2 and 3, and you've thought about how your employee performed during the evaluation period. Now, you take a deep breath and begin rating him or her.

As in most other areas of life, honesty is the best policy. Be as objective as possible. Be aware of factors that could bias your evaluations.

Sources of Bias in Evaluations

There are several factors that can cause managers to have difficulty making fair and objective judgments. In this section we discuss the most common.

We are usually aware of *personal prejudice*—at least in others. Personal prejudices can cause managers to evaluate employees more harshly or more favorably, sometimes without being aware of the influence of those personal feelings.

We can also be influenced by *cross-cultural bias*, assumptions that we make without allowing for the effects of cultural differences. In a way, it's almost the flip side of personal prejudice. A prejudice is based on assumptions about people whom you consider different in some way from you, while cross-cultural bias is essentially the assumption that all people are the same as you.

> *Cross-cultural bias* is a consequence of a person's expectations and assumptions about human behavior that don't take into consideration differences in culture that affect our beliefs, values, and behavior.

Mirroring, also known as the "like me" or "similar to me" bias, is the effect of feeling more favorably disposed toward people who are like us in some way—similar in such respects as personality, work habits, background, personal interests, likes and dislikes, social affiliations, politics, religion, and so on—and, conversely, to feel less comfortable around people who are less like us.

A similar bias is in play when we consciously or subconsciously compare one employee with another. It may be difficult not to compare the performance of two or more employees who do the same job or similar jobs, especially in areas such as sales, where there's a focus on goals and often a competitive atmosphere. If you have a stellar employee and some who are only very good, you might tend to grade the good employees a little lower than they deserve.

Another bias that may affect a manager's judgment is actually a pair/dichotomy—the *halo effect* and the *horns effect*. This is what happens when a manager downplays bad things an employee does because the employee is good in other areas (*halo effect*) or downplays good things an employee does because the employee is bad in other areas *(horns effect)*.

The ***halo effect*** and the ***horns effect*** are inappropriate generalizations from one area of a person's performance to all areas of his or her performance.

High potential error is a form of the halo effect. This is when a manager allows an employee's potential to positively influence the rating of his or her performance.

A bias similar to the halo effect and the horns effect is the *recency effect*. This is when a manager judges performance that's fresher in the memory as more important than earlier or long-term performance. It's natural for a manager to remember best what an employee has done most recently, so it's important to think back over the entire evaluation period and evaluate the employee's performance with greater balance. There may be legitimate reasons for a manager to base an evaluation more on recent performance than on earlier performance, such as when an employee has been improving. However, it's important not to be swayed if an employee is motivated to do his or her job better only because the time for performance appraisals is approaching.

In this context I should also mention the *first impression*

> The *recency effect* is a natural tendency to judge someone's performance based more on his or her most recent actions than on long-term performance.

error, which is the tendency of a manager to be influenced by an initial positive or negative judgment of an employee. Although it's true that people never get a second chance to make a first impression, be vigilant not to let any first impressions you have of your employees influence your ratings. Similar to the first impression error is the past performance error, which is when a manager allows an employee's poor or excellent performance in a previous evaluation period to color his or her judgment about how the employee has performed in the evaluation period in question.

A particular form of the halo/horns effect is called *attribution bias* or the *attributive error*. This is when a manager holds an employee responsible for performance problems, but attributes good performance to other people or to things for which the employee is not responsible. For example, if an employee misses an important project deadline, the manager considers it to be his or her fault, but if he or she makes an important deadline, the manager credits other employees for helping or somehow facilitating that success.

> *Attribution bias* is the tendency to attribute performance problems to factors under the employee's control and successes to external factors.

Finally, we should consider three forms of bias that may cause a manager to evaluate all of his or her employees inaccurately.

A manager who wants to be liked by his or her employees or to avoid conflict may tend to be lenient in evaluating them. He or she might rate them all as being above average in every area—in line with the *Lake Wobegon effect*—in hopes of not offending any of them. (Yes, it's possible that your employees are all above average, but probably not in every area of their job responsibilities.) On the

Starting with Average

To avoid rating your employees higher than they deserve, it may help to begin the evaluation on each item with the average rating, "meets expectations" (or whatever may be your midpoint). Then, decide if the employee does better than meeting expectations in that category or not as well. It is believed that when we start visually at the top of a scale it's more difficult psychologically to go down as far as would be appropriate. The same may be true of starting at the other end of the rating scale.

other hand, a manager who wants to maintain a reputation for being demanding may evaluate more strictly.

The third bias in this trio is called the *error of central tendency*. This, as you would guess from the label, is when a manager tends to rate employees as being closer to average than they deserve to be rated for their performance, avoiding more negative or positive judgments that might need justification.

The *error of central tendency* is the inclination to rate people toward the middle of a scale even though their performance warrants a higher or lower rating.

Let's end this section with a caution against intentional distortion of employee evaluations. "In addition to bias, flaws in the execution of an appraisal program can be destructive. For instance, managers may be downgrading their employees because high performance reviews would outstrip the department's budget for bonuses. Or, some managers may be using performance appraisals to achieve personal or departmental political goals, thus distorting assessments" (Dave Mote, "Performance Appraisal and Standards," *Encyclopedia of Business* [2nd Ed.], *www.referenceforbusiness.com/encyclopedia*). Any form of intentional distortion of employee evaluations is wrong, of course, and it's both unfair to the employees and dangerous in terms of the potential effects on performance management.

Maintain Balance

Being honest includes maintaining a balance that fairly represents the employee's performance. Don't focus only or primarily on areas for improvement. Recognize also areas in which the employee has performed well.

It may be easier for you to maintain an honest balance when discussing your evaluation with your employee if you simply follow the order of the items on the form, which should be prioritized according to the job functions and responsibilities. Simply go through the items and appraise each aspect of performance, good or bad.

Narratives

Your evaluation form should allow for narratives to accompany any ratings. If the evaluation consists of ratings alone, it's all about the past, since ratings provide no explanation, no guidance for the employee who needs to improve. The purpose of the narrative is to explain and support the ratings and provide guidance.

More Than Numbers

"Even if your appraisal form only calls for you to 'check a box,'" says Robert Bacal and Douglas Max in their book, *Perfect Phrases for Performance Reviews*, second edition (McGraw-Hill, 2011), "you generally can add additional comments to justify or explain the rating. In fact, *if the appraisal process is to have any value to the employee, you must provide more information than a numeric rating.*"

The first rule of writing narratives to accompany evaluations is simple: document everything. Don't say anything that you can't support with evidence. Have documentation for any specific incident you reference on the evaluation.

You've got a good start on writing the narratives if you've mentally reviewed the employee's performance over the evaluation period, as recommended a few pages earlier in this chapter, and jotted down notes about what you remember. You've also got the materials you've gathered.

Writing narratives is an art. You generally need to be specific but you also need to be brief. Narratives may also be known as narrative *essays*, although they're generally not long, or narrative *summaries*, although they may be more specific than one might expect of a summary. If your company provides standard evaluation forms, you may be required to fit a narrative within a box or on a few lines. It may also be that you're allowed as much space as you need. Keep in mind the purpose(s) of your narratives. Are they to justify the rating in case an employee complains about it? Maybe. Are they to explain the rating? Definitely. Are they to indicate what the employee should have done or not done, in addition to telling what happened or didn't happen? That depends on the situation. Are they to provide general guidance? Possibly. Your company may specify what is expected in a narrative or you may need to decide based on the conventions and expectations of your workplace culture.

Richard Gorham, president of *Leadership-Tools.com*, offers the following advice:

- You should comment on all goals as well as behavioral and/or performance factors. A rating is not enough. Explain how you came to your conclusion.
- Provide real on-the-job examples for all behavioral or performance expectations.

That seems like the ideal. You may not be able to do all that. If you've been communicating with your employees about their performance, you may not need to write as much as if you discuss performance only once a year.

The language you use is very important. Here are a few guidelines:

- Use objective language to describe performance.
- Focus on behaviors, on actions rather than attitudes or beliefs or whatever else may have motivated the behaviors.
- Avoid generalities and labels (e.g., "He's lazy," "She has a bad attitude," "He has a problem with authority figures," "She's a liar").

- Be specific and clear.
- Provide more details for ratings that are particularly low or high.

As guides to the language of performance appraisals, I can recommend the following books:

Perfect Phrases for Performance Reviews (2nd edition) by Douglas Max and Robert Bacal (McGraw-Hill, 2011)

Perfect Phrases for Documenting Employee Performance Problems by Anne Bruce (McGraw-Hill, 2005)

Finally, after you've written the narratives, take a moment to read them over—from the perspective of your employee. You may decide to tweak the wording. You probably won't find any reason to change the substance of your words, but you may reduce subjectivity and temper any negative emotions coming through in your words. It's all about making your points honestly without unnecessarily offending.

The Mean Standard

Communication consultant Meryl Runion—author of *Speak Strong, How to Say It: Performance Reviews* (with Janelle Brittain), and *Perfect Phrases for Managers and Supervisors*—says it best: "Say what you mean and mean what you say, without being mean when you say it."

Prepare for the Meeting
Make a Plan

As for any meeting, you should set an agenda for performance appraisal meetings. All you need is an outline or a checklist of what you want to cover, the essential points you want to make, and the key questions you want to ask. This will help you keep the meeting focused and make the most effective and efficient use of your time.

Keep in mind that the purpose of the appraisal meeting isn't only to share and discuss the employee's appraisal. It provides an opportunity for manager and employee to discuss performance issues, diagnose any problems, and propose and consider ideas for minimizing those problems.

Begin the meeting by briefly discussing the performance appraisal process in general and your goals: to help your employee perform his or her job better by discussing problems he or she may be experiencing and to express appreciation for his or her accomplishments and successes. You also want to find out how he or she feels, ease anxiety, and adjust erroneous expectations.

Then, plan to transition into discussing the evaluation. It's probably best to proceed from top to bottom, if the items on the form are organized logically. Otherwise, you might want to cover them in terms of the priorities of the employee's job functions and responsibilities. Whatever you do, don't begin with a long list of positives or a long list of negatives.

It's important to stay organized and on track, as with conducting any business meeting, but it's crucial to answer any questions your employee asks and to listen to whatever he or she says about the evaluation or related issues.

You may want to prepare the comments you intend to make about the evaluation—or especially those that you expect to be more difficult. Be prepared to offer suggestions for improving.

Be careful not to plan to hit a lot of points. You want to help your employee learn from the evaluation and improve, not overwhelm him or her with a long list of performance problems and weaknesses.

Plan Your Opening

Plan to start the meeting by putting your employee at ease. Otherwise, anxiety may distract him and her throughout the meeting and make discussion more difficult and emotional. Explain again the purposes and benefits of the appraisal meeting. If you've prepared notes, you won't have to rely on your memory and appear unprepared.

It's wise to plan to transition with more general questions to open the discussion. If you've given your employee some general questions in advance, as we suggested earlier in this chapter, you can use them as a good way to begin discussing his or her performance.

Anticipate Reactions

You should be prepared for however your employees react to the evaluation. Most of your employees are probably doing their jobs well enough, so they're likely to be happy or at least relieved to receive confirmation of what they believe and are interested in knowing how they can do their jobs better. However, if any of your employees are performing poorly or are anxious about the appraisal meeting and/or skeptical about the process and the benefits, you should prepare for dealing with their emotions.

They may become defensive, angry, argumentative, or sad. They may go silent. They may cry. Be prepared to pause in your discussion. Be prepared to remain calm, whatever happens. We get into specifics of employee reactions in Chapter 5.

Mad, Sad, Glad, and Scared

"Think about the employee's likely reaction to the appraisal," Richard C. Grote advises in *The Complete Guide to Performance Appraisal* (AMA-COM, 1996, p. 155). He then adds, "A useful device for understanding emotional reactions is to recognize that there are only four emotions: mad, sad, glad, and scared...." That may or may not be true, but he notes that those emotions can be expressed in various ways. Anger can make an employee hostile and/or bitter. An employee who is sad may become depressed, uncommunicative, and closed to suggestions and may cry. An employee who seems glad to receive an unfavorable appraisal may be in denial.

Ideally, nothing that you put in the evaluation or say during your meeting should come as a surprise to the employee. Employees generally know how they're doing, how well they're handling their job responsibilities. If not, then your responsibility as their manager is to provide feedback throughout the evaluation period, not only in formal performance appraisals.

Nothing should come as a surprise to the employee—but that

doesn't mean that the employee will not surprise you. Be prepared.

> **No Big Surprises**
> As you're evaluating your employees, if you get the feeling that any rating you're giving or anything you're writing in a narrative might surprise the employee, make a note to yourself to be particularly diplomatic in discussing that point—and another note to communicate better with the employee during the next evaluation period.

Prepare to Ask Questions

The performance appraisal meeting is not for you to present your evaluation of the employee. It must be a time of open communication. That means allowing and encouraging the employee to talk about his or her job performance. You can't waste this opportunity for true discussion.

The best way to encourage employees to talk is by asking questions—good questions. OK, so what makes a question "good"?

Let's consider three types of questions.

A *closed* question is one intended to elicit an answer of "Yes" or "No." For example, "Have you finished the report?" or "Has the team started the improvement project?" In essence, a closed question is a statement that ends with a question mark. Our two example questions could also be worded as "You have finished the report" and "The team has started the improvement project" and you could respond by either nodding or shaking your head. If you've ever played the game of 20 questions, you know how long it can take to get information through yes/no questions.

> A *closed* question elicits an answer of "Yes" or "No." In function it's basically a statement that ends with a question mark.

A little more productive is the *directional* question. Whereas the closed question offers only two options, yes and no, the directional question presents two or more options and calls for a choice. For example, "Where do you want to meet, in my office or in yours?" or "Who has the file now—Peter, Paul, or Mary?" The options may be worded a little differently, such as "Which of the project team members has the most Six Sigma experience?" In all three examples, the question presents options and the answer chooses between or among them. (Of course, you could answer with an option not presented by the question; the directional question simply indicates some directions, not necessarily all the possible directions an answer could take.)

> A ***directional*** question presents two or more options and elicits an answer that makes a choice among those options.

The third and last question we'll consider here is the *open* or *open-ended* question. As the name indicates, this type of question is open to a wide variety of answers. For example, "What do you like about your job?" The question leaves you free to answer in any way, at least within reason. You could answer, "The pay" or "The lunch room" or "My purple pen," for example.

> An ***open*** question places no explicit restrictions on the answer. Open questions engage the person answering in a more active role.

Now, let's consider the effects of asking these three types of questions. The following three questions all target the same area but in different ways:

- "Do you like your job?" (closed)
- "What do you like more about your job, working on projects or training new employees?" (directional)
- "How do you feel about your job and why?" (open)

The first question will get an answer of "Yes" or "No." The second question will get an answer of "working on projects" or "training new employees." The third question will get an answer ... that can lead to a good discussion.

Some people use the term *high-gain* for certain open questions. High-gain questions go beyond normal open questions in that they are intended to elicit not just a broader response but a thoughtful and thorough answer. They may be effective in getting a person to imagine, to consider possibilities, to speculate, and to think outside the box.

A high-gain question enables you to gain the most information in the shortest time. Asking a series of open and closed questions may give you a quantity of information, but it could prove to be a very time-consuming process.

For example:

Low-gain questions:

"Did you talk with someone in Human Resources?"

"Did you complete the paperwork?"

High-gain question:

"What steps have you taken so far?"

Proper questioning is important. Prepare some questions in advance to engage your employee and stimulate candid, honest, and productive discussion. Consider the following examples:

- What aspects of your job do you find most interesting?
- What do you consider your most important achievement in the past year?
- How can I help you finish your reports on time?
- How would you suggest that we improve communication in our department?
- What do you think might have caused your performance to suffer?

Notice that these questions are general; you could have occasion to ask them of almost any employee. Don't plan questions in detail and you shouldn't necessarily use all of the questions you prepare with every employee. If you read questions from a list, it will seem mechanical to your employee. Also, you may find it more difficult to depart from the list and ask spontaneous questions. Follow-up questions may be the most important because they start from something that your employee says. Prepare enough basic questions so you feel ready to think on your feet. Exhibit 4-1 summarizes these question types and their purposes.

No Aggressive Questions

There's a type of question that you should avoid—the *aggressive* question. An aggressive question expresses a negative feeling, such as disbelief, disrespect, disdain, and so on.

- "Why in the world did you do that?"
- "What would ever make you believe that it was OK to leave early?"

Often a question is aggressive not because of the words, but because of the tone. For example, the question, "Why do you believe that?" when asked in a neutral or concerned tone is a simple request for an explanation, while the same question asked in an aggressive tone says essentially, "How could you be so stupid as to believe that?" The aggressive question is not intended to get an answer; it's intended to express a negative feeling.

Review Development Needs

Prepare to talk with your employee about his or her development needs. Identify skills and competencies that may improve performance. However, refrain from getting into discussing ways to

Question Types	Result	Purpose
Closed Questions	Get yes or no answers	Useful for making decisions or getting facts
Directional Questions	Choice among two or more options	Good for allowing a choice but limiting the freedom to choose
Open Questions	Full sentence answers	Helps to gain a point of view and broader perspective on the question
High-Gain Questions	Speculative and creative answers and further questions	Used to get a feel for the other person's thinking and to tap into his or her creativity

Exhibit 4-1. Question Types and Purposes

meet development needs. That discussion should take place at another time.

A performance appraisal meeting is in some ways like most other meetings. You have an agenda, your list of things to cover, and that agenda should include a plan to schedule a follow-up meeting to discuss your employee's personal development.

What should happen next? Performance plan, career development, additional assignment, promotion? Where do you and the employee go from here?

Why should you not discuss personal development at the performance appraisal meeting? Because that's a subject that deserves a meeting devoted to personal development.

The linking of performance appraisal and personal development is "an unholy alliance," according to Jeremy Francis of Jeremy Francis HR. For most employees, he notes, the annual performance appraisal meeting is the only time when they will be discussing their personal development and their career path in any detail with their manager. In a way, "their personal agenda of career development, job satisfaction, and personal development" is just appended to the discussion of performance.

Francis gives good reasons why the atmosphere of the performance appraisal meeting is "not at all appropriate" for discussing personal development. Basically, it's "because the emphasis and focus of each should be different." He offers the following contrast:

Performance Appraisal Discussion	Personal Development Discussion
• Led by the manager	• Led by the employee
• Based on results and past performance	• Based on skills and talents and future growth
• Judgmental	• Developmental
• Focused on the needs of the organization	• Focused on the needs of the employee
• Related to pay and compensation	• Related to the employee's career

Source: Jeremy Francis, "Performance Appraisal and Personal Development—The Unholy Alliance," *jeremyfrancishr.com*

So, prepare to touch on your employee's development needs as they arise naturally in your discussion of his or her performance, but to defer discussion of development. Schedule a follow-up meeting with only personal development on the agenda.

5 Conducting Performance Appraisal Meetings

N ow it's time to meet with the employee you've evaluated. You're ready with the evaluation form you've completed, your supporting documentation, the employee's performance plan for the evaluation period, and notes from others about his or her performance. Just before the meeting, you reviewed the evaluation so it's fresh in your mind. You're ready to discuss the ratings and the facts supporting each rating.

Before each meeting, remind yourself of the purpose: to improve performance. Repeat the "mantra" suggested by the words of Robert Bacal quoted in Chapter 4: "The review process is a partnership. ... It's a problem-solving process. ... It's about looking forward, not looking backward."

Preliminaries

Make sure that the room is appropriate for creating a comfortable atmosphere. The layout should be informal. This is more difficult if you need to be accessing computer files, but try to minimize the presence of a desk between you and your employee. Should you

> **No Surprises**
> "If I had to choose two words to guide managers in the performance appraisal process," Robert Bacal says in his book, *Performance Management* (McGraw-Hill, 1999), "it would be 'no surprises.'" As he explains, "Rarely is there a need to discuss things at the appraisal meeting that haven't been discussed during the year." As a result, "once employees realize you're not going to spring surprises on them in the appraisal meeting, they start to work with you and feel more comfortable." The bottom line: "If there are surprises, something has gone wrong."

provide refreshments? That depends on the culture of your work unit. It makes sense to at least have water available.

Assemble in advance all the documents, notes, and files you need to support your evaluation. Don't wait until the last minute; you're more likely to miss something. In fact, it's wise to review the evaluation forms and your notes prior to the meeting. Employees quickly realize when their manager has not prepared adequately for their performance review. Employees will usually get a sense of the amount of time and effort you put into the appraisal process. Your preparation shows respect for your employee, who should appreciate it. (It's good for employees to feel appreciated—and it should make your job easier!)

You need to be familiar with organizational policies pertaining to performance appraisals and, in particular, to meeting with employees to discuss evaluations. You don't want to complicate your life by doing something wrong.

Bring paper and a pen or pencil so you can take notes during the meeting. Points may come up that you'll want to check later or you may remember something you forgot when filling out the evaluation form. You'll also want to document any issues the employee raises.

In addition, taking notes on what your employee says makes it easier for you to refrain from interrupting and then later you can refer back to points you want to pursue. There's also a psychological benefit. If you take notes on what your employee is saying, it shows that you're taking it (and him or her) seriously.

Finally, when you're ready to begin the meeting, remember to turn off your cell phone and/or pager and close the door. Avoiding interruptions makes for a better meeting and it shows respect for your employee and for the performance appraisal process.

Beginning the Meeting

Some managers generally like to begin any meeting with a bang, to jump immediately into the agenda. That's not a good idea with any one-on-one meeting with an employee, especially if it's for a performance appraisal.

You should spend the first two or three minutes setting the mood so both of you feel comfortable and ready to work together. Start by reiterating the purpose of the meeting. Explain briefly that you will be sharing the evaluation results and the two of you will be discussing them, focusing on how you two can work together to improve performance.

Starting Questions

Robert Bacal suggests starting with talking about feelings, with two types of questions. You could start with your employee: "Tom, usually employees feel a little nervous about these meetings. How are you feeling right now?" You could also start with yourself: "I always worry that these meetings are going to be difficult. I try to remind myself that we've done all our homework, so there won't be any surprises." (*Performance Management*)

Keep small talk to a minimum, since appraisals should be taken seriously, but it's important for both of you to feel comfortable enough to collaborate. The atmosphere should be amicable, positive, and open.

Your body language should be open. This would include making eye contact, keeping your arms relaxed and open (not folded), and nodding to affirm certain points. The employee may be attentive to your body language, especially to indications that you are not open to whatever he or she is saying. Closed body language includes having your arms folded and/or your shoulders or legs turned away, and being easily distracted.

I suggested in Chapter 4 that you prepare some preliminary questions and comments that would allow you and your employee to ease into your agenda. Actually, they should be the first item on your agenda. It's important to get the employee talking as soon as possible, so he or she feels more at ease engaging in discussion with you.

You might start with a question like "How do you feel you've been doing this past year, in general?" Then you can shape your transition into the agenda according to the response. As you listen to the words, be attentive as well to the tone and body language.

It's usually best to begin on a positive note, even if the evaluation results are not so good. You must be honest in your evaluation, of course, but you also want your employee to be emotionally open to the evaluation results.

Beware of being overly positive—or overly negative. First, the employee may not believe what you say or at least be unsure or even confused. Try to start with a balance of positive and negative consistent with the evaluation results, but lead with the most positive points and follow with the big negative points. Then, as you review the results with your employee, you should try to present a mix of positives and negatives consistent with the results, so the tone doesn't become overly negative or overly positive.

Discussing the Evaluation

Managers generally want to be efficient when they run meetings. However, you should treat performance appraisal meetings differently. An appraisal meeting should take the form of a dialogue between you and your employee. It's about an effective meeting of the minds, not efficiency. It's about maintaining a spirit of collaboration as much as getting through your agenda.

How you share the results of your evaluation is critical. The employee must accept the process or the meeting is a waste of time and effort. You should know each of your employees at least well enough to have a sense of how to communicate with them and understand what they're communicating through their body language. Use what you know to keep your employee involved in the appraisal meeting and actively engaged.

Be careful with your body language. In particular, don't keep looking at your watch or the clock. Your employee is likely to take that as a sign of impatience or even a signal to talk less so you can finish the meeting sooner.

If the meeting runs long and you've got something coming up on your schedule that can't be delayed, you can adjourn and continue at another time. It's important for appraisal meetings to be a good experience for your employees if you want to improve communications. If you act like the meetings and your employees are less important to you than whatever you've got next, you may be paying a high price in performance management for the little time you save hurrying appraisal meetings.

Starting with the Bottom Line

Begin by giving your general assessment or summary rating, depending on the form of evaluation. Whether the appraisal is all good or not, it's best to start with the bottom line.

Keep it simple: "I think that you've generally done very well in meeting your objectives," for example, or "I've given you an overall rating of 'fair but needs improvement.'" Then, follow with a few of the most salient points to support that assessment. As mentioned above, balance positive points and negative points consistent with the evaluation results.

Don't spend much time on this summation. Be sensitive to the employee's body language and attentive to any indication that he or she is ready to move on from the general assessment into particulars.

Going Item by Item

Reviewing performance evaluations can be basically straightforward. As mentioned in Chapter 4, it's probably best to go through the results item by item. You can do this in three steps.

First, state the objective or the category or competency, depending on the form of the evaluation, and then give your assessment or rating. Pause for a moment.

Next, explain the basis for your assessment on that item, which may be a list of critical events or a narrative. Be specific. It may not be necessary to provide dates, times, and places for each example, but you should have them on the evaluation form and provide them if the employee questions an example.

Then invite the employee to respond, with a question such as "Would you agree with that assessment?" or "How do you feel about how you performed [with regard to that objective *or* in terms of that competency item]?" Your question should be general, not about a specific instance you've mentioned or you can expect that the discussion will digress.

No Absolutes

Avoid making extreme comments (e.g., "You've been completely irresponsible") or using absolutes (e.g., never, always). It's easy for an employee to attack such statements: he or she needs to offer only one example to the contrary to disprove your point.

Maintain a calm, positive tone of voice. Your demeanor should be consistent with what you are saying. If you smile as you mention a negative point or fail to smile when you say something good, you're sending a mixed message.

If you have reason to praise or compliment the employee, do so, of course. (Why would you not recognize good performance?) However, don't go to extremes. That may embarrass your employee and cause him or her to wonder if there's bad news coming.

It's generally smart to follow your evaluation form as a script. Deviate from it only to answer questions that the evaluation form doesn't address. You should not need to come up with explanations or examples that aren't on the form. If you mention something you should have included on the form, make a note of it.

Show that you are interested in helping your employee perform better and in discussing the evaluation, but don't insist on discussion if the employee shows no interest. Simply go through

Behaviors, Not Labels

If you say things like "You've got a bad attitude" or "You're lazy," you aren't helping your employees improve. It seems like an opinion, a label you've applied. Give examples of behaviors, such as "You've gotten into arguments over trivial matters" or "You've been avoiding work responsibilities on your project team." Deal with facts and avoid generalities.

the results item by item, reading from the form and pausing occasionally to allow and encourage the employee to respond.

How often should you pause? It's not so much a question of time but rather of the amount of information you convey. A rough guide would be to pause after you give the evaluation for an item and then again after each piece of supporting evidence.

How long should you wait for a response? There's no magic number, but I'd suggest waiting between 5 and 10 seconds. Wait long enough to allow a response, of course, and a little longer so the silence makes the employee feel a little uncomfortable. Vary the wait time so the process doesn't feel mechanical. If a wait time of 5 to 10 seconds doesn't get any response after the first half-dozen attempts, shorten the time so you don't become frustrated.

Some people believe that a manager who points out a weakness should offer the employee suggestions for improvement. This seems like sound advice, but follow it with caution. If an employee is weak in numerous areas, your constructive criticisms may seem like lecturing. Also, if you want to encourage the employee to think about his or her performance issues, you may be missing out on some opportunities to do so. It may sometimes be better to consider asking the employee questions like "How could you do X better?"

Another potential problem with offering constructive criticism is that a manager might naturally slip into making comparisons, e.g., "You could try doing ... like Sarah" or "Have you noticed how Pablo does ...?" That's dangerous. Never compare one employee to another or even give the impression of doing that. You're likely to cause the employee in question to react by pointing out ways in which he or she is different—and then the discussion goes off track and nowhere good. You may also be conveying the message that you don't care about individual differences among your employees. In addition, you may also cause the employee to feel resentment toward the other employees.

I should mention here the question of using input from third parties, such as coworkers, customers, and other managers. Should you be prepared to cite names, places, and times as you would for instances of behavior that you witnessed personally? On the one hand, if you mention something that came from a third party, it may seem suspect if it's anonymous (e.g., "Somebody told me that …"). The result could be denial and resistance. On the other hand, if you identify your sources, the employee could question that person's credibility and/or motives and the discussion could get sidetracked. Also, your employees may become reluctant to tell you anything about problem behavior they witness if they fear retaliation from the employee in question.

If something comes up during the meeting that you realize you should have included in one of your narratives, make a note of it. (You should be taking notes during your discussion, so this would be just one more.) Then, after the meeting, you should revise the evaluation form.

Asking Questions

Allow and even encourage the employee to express how he or she feels about the evaluation. You may learn about the causes underlying performance problems and get insights into dealing with them.

To be most effective, you should ask open questions, questions that elicit answers beyond "Yes" or "No." (I'm using the word "question" loosely here to refer to words intended to get information. It would include such statements as "Tell me about …")

Ask high-gain questions. These questions encourage the employee to think more broadly. High-gain questions are more likely to stimulate conversation. Examples of high-gain questions would be "Tell me more about that" and "What would it be like if you had the support you needed?" and "Tell me about a time when things were going particularly well." You could ask, "Does this assessment seem fair to you?" and follow up with "Why?" or "Why not?" and then "Would you have done anything differently this year?"

Not all questions are good for a discussion of performance appraisal, of course. *Directive* questions generally discourage discussion or even thinking. For example, "Do you agree, then, that your behavior was unsatisfactory?" is not so much a question as a request to agree. Even questions such as "So, have we covered everything?" or "Are we ready to move on to the next item?" can seem to the employee as statements to which he or she is simply expected to agree.

In Chapter 4, I recommended that you prepare questions that you expect would be appropriate. In the course of the meeting, other questions will come to mind, as well. When that happens, pause briefly to consider how the question would sound from that particular employee's perspective in that context. I think we've all asked questions that we immediately or later wish we had phrased a little differently—or not asked at all.

Listening

Perhaps the biggest mistake that many managers make in appraisal meetings is talking too much and not listening enough. I've advised asking questions. Here I advise listening—actively.

It's important to allow the employee to react to the performance appraisal. If he or she has done a self-evaluation, ask about that. You could compare the two evaluations item by item and then allow the employee to explain any discrepancies between the evaluations.

When the employee talks, listen, listen, listen. Use *active listening*. This means participating in the communication process actively and taking responsibility for the message being communicated.

Active listening means using both ears and body language. Listen more than you speak. When you speak, use phrases like "Tell me more" or "I understand how you feel." Your purpose is to open up conversation rather than dominate the meeting.

To engage your employee, do the following:

- Focus on him or her.
- Listen to both the facts and the emotions behind them.
- Observe body language and tone of voice.
- Provide cues that you are paying attention, such as nodding or saying things like "Yes" or "I understand."
- Ask open-ended questions.
- Paraphrase what your employee says.
- Show empathy.
- Demonstrate caring without being or seeming to be patronizing.
- Exercise patience.

Don't interrupt, although you want to make sure the discussion is not sidetracked by irrelevant topics.

A key aspect of active listening is *empathy*. Put yourself in the shoes of your employee. The appraisal meeting can be stressful, especially when it involves corrective action. If you are really listening actively, you are naturally more likely to feel empathetic.

Dealing with Emotions

Meeting with the boss to discuss performance can be very difficult for many employees. Be prepared for various reactions.

It's not always possible to engage an employee in a discussion of his or her performance. If an employee doesn't respond to your questions, it's important not to become apprehensive or impatient. Continue with reporting the evaluation results. Tell your employee that he or she should feel free to come and discuss with you any questions that arise after the meeting.

An employee may become hostile. If that happens, remain calm, objective, and focused on the appraisal. Let the employee vent. Don't react with anger or hostility. Don't become defensive and argue. Listen to what the employee says and try to determine why he or she is reacting in that way, but don't try to discuss any-thing or expect to convince the employee of anything while he or she is angry. Don't try to reason with someone who doesn't seem open to discussing reasonably.

Whatever the employee may say in anger, remain profes-sional. Take notes on any points he or she makes that could be worth pursuing later. Jot down just a few words for each point, enough so you can understand your notes later, but not so much as to distract you from what the employee is saying. It's crucial not to give the impression that you're not paying attention. If he or she asks what you're doing, reply simply, "You're raising some good points that I don't want to forget."

When the employee calms down, you can discuss the points that you noted. Say, "I'd like to talk about some of the points you made. Where do you want to begin?" You could also choose points to discuss. Don't try to respond to every point. When peo-ple get angry, they can say a lot of things that don't really matter to them. If a point is important to the employee, he or she is likely to repeat it.

During a tough appraisal meeting, it's important to stay cool and collected and to spend more time listening than talking. Naturally, avoid arguing. Using reflecting skills like paraphrasing what the employee is saying can help you maintain control, gather information, and defuse potential conflict.

Sometimes people react to criticism or what they perceive as criticism by becoming defensive. You can make this less likely by beginning with positive feedback. If the employee becomes defen-sive, try to shift the focus from the past to the future, to his or her potential to perform better.

Disagreeing

It may happen that your employee doesn't agree with something you say. That's to be expected if you are encouraging open com-munication. It may also happen that you don't agree with him or her on some point.

What if you disagree about how you rated your employee? Most ratings are subjective. Be flexible about minor differences. A rating will probably not cause an employee to improve. What will make a difference is the discussion that the performance appraisal generates and the effect of communication between manager and employee. It's a waste of time and energy to argue about whether an employee merits a "meets expectations" or an "exceeds expectations" on one item out of many. Arguing over a small point like that makes no sense in the big scheme of things and makes the meeting more difficult, so the dispute affects much more than that single point on the evaluation form. If you and your employee have a difference of opinion, it should not be about the result, the assessment, but rather about the reasons, your difference of perspective.

If the employee makes a good case for a better rating, change the rating. If the employee cannot show sufficient cause to change it, leave it. Say that you appreciate his or her perspective but you disagree with it. (Don't feel obligated to change it on the spot. Make a note of what the employee says and promise to get back to him or her as soon as possible. You may want to check out the information and you may want to think about how to adjust the evaluation and/or revise the narrative. It also may be that your organization uses computerized evaluation forms, so making changes at the meeting isn't an option.)

Note the disagreement and the employee's position. In fact, you should be documenting all substantive comments by the employee, just as you would be diligent in taking minutes in any business meeting.

It's important to try to resolve issues that arise. However, it's also important to avoid digressions. Don't get off track. It's a question of balancing the value of open communication with the need to cover the agenda.

Agree to disagree. Document any points of unresolved disagreement. If it's about the performance appraisal, make your employee's position part of the official record. If it's about other matters—such as revising objectives, getting more resources/ training, and personal development—set it aside for later, when you meet to discuss personal development and to set objectives.

If you two disagree on some point and fail to resolve your differences, offer your employee the option of writing his or her position and perspective for the performance appraisal file. This may be part of performance appraisal procedures in your organization. It's a good idea—and smart from the legal perspective.

Diagnosing Difficulties

"Determining the extent to which the employee has achieved the objectives … is probably the most trivial or unimportant part of the appraisal process," said Robert Bacal in his book, *Performance Management* (McGraw-Hill, 1999). "The guts of the process—the part that will contribute to better performance—is the diagnosis." Although we could quibble about "most trivial or unimportant," it's true that diagnosing the difficulties is indeed "the guts of the process."

As you and the employee discuss the evaluation results, you will naturally be talking about causes of performance problems. As you do, avoid blaming—whether it's you blaming the employee or the employee blaming others. Keep the focus on the future, on resolving performance problems.

As a manager, you're accustomed to solving problems. Resist the impulse to do so here. Resist the temptation to assume responsibility for solving any performance problems. You don't need to have all the answers on how to improve or how to move to the next career step. The employee is responsible for his or her performance and should be able to have some specific suggestions or to raise issues that you may not have considered. Show that you're willing to help the employee solve his or her issues. Ask, "What do I need to do as manager to help you improve?"

What you want to do here is get the employee to start thinking about how he or she could be performing better. You should then, at the end of the appraisal meeting, schedule a meeting to continue discussing performance issues, to talk about personal development, and to set objectives. Engaging in some little diagnosis of performance difficulties during the appraisal meeting is taking a first step in the direction of the matters to be discussed at that next meeting. Of course, whatever ideas and suggestions and questions arise during this diagnosis, you should write down and save for that meeting.

Be careful! This is a slippery slope. A discussion of performance issues can easily lead into discussing personal development. Keep in mind that the appraisal meeting is not the time or place to discuss development needs or make any plans.

Final Matters

After you and your employee have reviewed and discussed the evaluation, you should be ready to close the meeting. Although we may not agree with the sweeping generalization by Shakespeare, "All's well that ends well," much of the real effect on performance comes from how the appraisal meeting ends.

Closing the Meeting

Show that you've listened attentively to the employee by repeating the points that he or she made about the evaluation. If the employee corrects you on any of the points (even if it's not really a correction), add the correction to your notes.

Review what you and your employee have decided to do and what you've decided to meet later to discuss. You should get a sense that your employee is committed to improving his or her performance, thinking about setting objectives for the next evaluation period, and discussing personal development plans. Depending on your procedure, that may include asking your employee to draft a set of objectives and/or plans for personal development.

Then there are the formalities, depending on the performance appraisal procedures in your organization. You may be required to ask the employee to sign and date the appraisal form to acknowledge that the discussion occurred. You may be required to give the appraisal to the employee at that time.

It may be that you will take care of the paperwork after the meeting. This would include getting from your employee a formal expression of disagreement or explanation to accompany the evaluation if he or she has decided to submit a document.

End the meeting on a positive note. Thank your employee and show that you appreciate his or her time and effort in actively participating in the meeting. (If the participation was less than active, you should word your comment appropriately. It's not wise to end the meeting with a comment that the employee will take as a sarcastic dig.)

Following Up

Assemble all your notes and other paperwork related to agreements reached in the meeting. Turn in the final appraisal. Most organizations keep documentation of performance appraisal meetings in their personnel files. You may be required to sign whatever documents you submit and have the employee sign them as well. Even if it's not required, it's a good policy to keep a copy of all documents for your own files.

It may be good to schedule follow-up actions as soon as possible after the meeting. This would include scheduling a meeting to discuss personal development plans and to set objectives for the next evaluation period; you may also be scheduling a separate meeting for the objectives.

Finally, schedule other matters that you offered or promised or decided to do. It's easy to forget when you have so many things to do—including performance appraisal meetings with other employees.

6 Legal Issues in Performance Management

C hapters 2, 3, 4, and 5 have covered the essentials of the Plan, Do, Check, React performance management cycle—Plan and Check. Before moving on to the React and Do phases, we need to consider legal issues.

There are two major reasons for putting this chapter on legal issues here. The first is that, whatever managers will do under the heading of "performance management," it will most probably include evaluating their employees and meeting with them to discuss those evaluations. The second reason is that evaluations and performance appraisal meetings generate documentation—and legal cases are based on evidence, much of which consists of documents.

However, to state the obvious, legal issues are important throughout the performance appraisal process and in performance management in general.

A Little Common Sense

You don't need to be an expert on employment law to avoid many of the legal problems that could arise out of performance management in general and performance appraisals in particular. You simply need to be systematic, objective, ethical, careful, and sensitive to your employees.

Take Precautions with Procedures

The procedures for your performance appraisals should come from the human resources department, and they should be legally sound. Whether that's the case in your situation or not, you should be aware of some important precautions.

Performance appraisal procedures should:

- Be uniform for all employees within the organization or at least within the work unit
- Be communicated formally to all employees
- Make the appraisal results accessible to all employees
- Provide all employees with information about their performance deficiencies
- Provide all employees with opportunities to improve their performance

Focus on Job Performance

The performance appraisal must be focused on the employee's specific job functions and responsibilities and how the employee has performed that job. That just makes sense: it's an appraisal of *job performance.*

In an excellent book chapter, "Current Legal Issues in Performance Appraisal" (in J. W. Smither (Ed.), *Performance Appraisal: State-of-the-Art Methods for Performance Management,* Jossey-Bass, 1998), attorney Stanley B. Malos offers the following recommendations for performance appraisal criteria.

- Ensure that the criteria are "job-related or based on job analysis."
- Limit the criteria to matters that are "within the control" of the employee.
- Relate the criteria to "specific functions, not global assessments."
- Make the criteria as objective as possible.
- Base the criteria "on behaviors rather than traits."

- Communicate the criteria to the employee.

Evaluate performance, not attitude. And never use the word "attitude" when writing performance reviews. Employment attorneys and courts have often viewed that as a code word concealing discrimination. Any vague statements about an employee's demeanor could be interpreted as discriminatory.

Treat Your Employees Equally

This is a matter of being fair. For the same job responsibilities, the same expectations apply to all employees doing that job. For the same level of job performance, the same treatment (rewards, recognition, disciplinary actions, or termination) apply to all employees.

Of course, employees are not all the same, performing the same job in the same way. Yet the principle applies.

Here a less simplistic evaluation system could give you an advantage. If you rate several employees doing the same job as "good," you could be expected to reward them equally and coach them equally. But if you rate each employee more precisely, with X objectives for a specific job function, then it's very unlikely that any two of those employees would deserve the same rating on every one of those X objectives. So, you may decide to reward each of them differently, and coach each of them a little differently. As long as you reward according to merit and coach according to need, it's fair.

Conduct Performance Appraisals at Least Annually

Performance appraisals are central to performance management. Therefore, you should be formally evaluating your employees regularly, at least once a year, although every six months or even quarterly might be more appropriate. Decide on the frequency that would be most effective in your situation and an appropriate investment of time and energy.

If your organization requires annual performance appraisals, you could hold less formal one-on-one meetings with your employees in the interim. Often annual appraisals are more difficult because they happen only once a year, so there's a lot at stake

> **Once a Year?!**
> Imagine running a business and doing the books—balance sheet, cash flow statement, etc.—only once a year. That would be crazy! But how many organizations and their managers talk about their employees (their "human resources") being essential to success ... and yet "do the books" on their employees only once a year?

and a long time to cover—and because managers and employees can "get rusty" between appraisals so the experience is naturally more difficult. Interim meetings can make the annual process easier and more effective.

By "performance appraisal," we mean a more or less formal process. However, as we discuss later, it's probably wise to be always evaluating your employees informally and communicating with them regularly about how they are doing their jobs. Continuous communication is essential to good performance management.

However often you decide to do performance appraisals, you should schedule them as regularly as possible and, again, treat all of your employees fairly. It's easy to procrastinate on more difficult tasks—and that's certainly true for appraisals. Managers may not mind meeting with their best employees, but just not find the time or energy to meet with others. That's unwise in terms of performance management, since the employees who have more performance problems need at least as much help as the others, and it's unwise in terms of the law.

Put It in Writing

Put as much of the performance appraisal process and the results in writing as possible. Document and record.

Document your procedures and then follow them. Doing so makes it all the more likely you will remain focused on job responsibilities and performance objectives and you will be treating all employees with the same responsibilities and objectives equally.

Record the appraisal results and keep those records. They may be only paper, but in the event of grievances or other legal procedures, they could be the hard evidence that saves your assets.

Communicate with Your Employees

Give each employee a copy of the results of his or her appraisal. Even if you've discussed the evaluation during the appraisal meeting, offer to answer any questions they might have about those results.

Keep Employee Records Confidential

It should not be necessary to remind you to keep all employee records confidential. You probably would never even consider sharing the contents of an employee's file with other employees, but you should also avoid talking about any aspects of the work performance of any employee with any other employee.

It's Tough, but It's Your Responsibility

Not many managers are comfortable about meeting with an employee with serious performance problems and being totally honest about deficiencies. But it's your responsibility.

To shirk that responsibility and avoid the discomfort by giving an inadequate employee an adequate or even good appraisal is unfair to the employee, of course. How can an employee work to improve if he or she is unaware that improvement is needed and expected?

But trying to avoid the responsibility to be honest with an employee about his or her poor performance could also result in legal liability for the organization if the employee is terminated. Even if the organization states clearly in its employee handbook that employment is "at will" and its employees "can be terminated at any time for any reason or for no reason at all," it's not free from liability. Employees who have been disciplined or terminated have won jury awards and out-of-court settlements against organizations based on claims that they didn't know their performance wasn't meeting expectations.

Organizations that terminate employees without first communicating with them about their poor performance and allowing them time to improve their deficiencies are taking a huge risk, since juries are likely to consider that lack of communication and opportunity to be unfair and improper conduct, even if the organization did not actually break any laws. It can be an expensive way for a manager to learn to take responsibility for being candid and honest with his or her employees, no matter how uncomfortable the manager may feel.

Don't Set Employees Up to Fail

There are legal risks if a manager does not follow the proper procedures for disciplining and terminating an employee. There may also be legal risks if a manager acts in such a way as to encourage employees to fail.

When employees don't meet expectations, a manager should always consider whether he or she is doing anything that might be contributing to those performance problems. That's just smart performance management.

When employees have a manager who is supportive, they tend to work harder to perform better, to make the most of their potential because they feel their manager values them. If they perform poorly, their manager is likely to react by trying to understand the factors affecting performance negatively and then helping the employees remedy their problems.

However, sometimes when there are performance problems, managers seem to decide that some of their employees are capable of doing better and some are not. They may show confidence in the "good employees" by being supportive of them and be less supportive of the "bad employees" and more controlling, judging them to be unlikely to perform adequately, at least not without close supervision.

Two organizational behaviorists who have studied this phenomenon have labeled it the "set-up-to-fail syndrome." Jean-François Manzoni and Jean-Louis Barsoux explain in their article, "How Bosses Create Their Own Poor Performers: The Set-Up-to-Fail Syndrome" (*Harvard Business Review*, March–April 1998), that some managers categorize their employees as being either in or out:

Members of the in-group are considered the trusted collaborators and therefore receive more autonomy, feedback, and expressions of confidence from their bosses. The boss–subordinate relationship for this group is one of mutual trust and reciprocal influence. Members of the out-group, on the other hand, are regarded more as hired hands and are managed in a more formal, less personal way, with more emphasis on rules, policies, and authority.

In reaction to this treatment, the "members of the out-group" essentially give up. As Manzoni and Barsoux explain, "when people perceive disapproval, criticism, or simply a lack of confidence and appreciation, they tend to shut down." The result? "Subordinates simply stop giving their best."

OK, this difference in treatment between the "in-group" and the "out-group" is bad performance management, but is it illegal discrimination? We all know that anybody can sue anybody for any reason at any time. Treat all of your employees fairly, allow them all the opportunity to perform well, use performance appraisal to find ways to help all your employees succeed and not as a reason to treat some as winners and some as losers. You'll be practicing smart performance management—and not be taking unnecessary risks with the legal system.

Discrimination

Many court cases have shown over the years, even large and otherwise ethical companies have erred in making promotion and salary decisions and, over the long run, with large groups of employees, have been found to statistically discriminate against minorities, women, and people in other protected classes.

Generally, this is the result not of racism, sexism, or agism, but simply of poor corporate guidance in training managers on how to avoid such bias. In some organizations, however, patterns of discrimination have not been inadvertent but result from corporate cultures that emphasize certain norms and stereotypes that are, in fact, discriminatory.

You may have seen these norms in action or you may have

sensed them as undercurrents in a corporate culture. They have been applied in hiring, promotion, salary, and termination decisions in many organizations. Just because they have been practiced by so many for so long, doesn't mean they are either true or legal.

Here are some of the laws intended to prevent this type of discrimination.

- **Title VII of the Civil Rights Act of 1964 (Title VII)**
  - Makes it illegal to discriminate on the basis of race, color, sex, religion, or national origin.
  - You cannot use performance appraisal procedures to perpetuate discrimination.

- **Equal Pay Act of 1963**
  - Makes gender-based differences in pay for equal work illegal, with limited exceptions.
  - Performance appraisal results may be used to justify these exceptions, such as for merit-pay differences.

- **Disparate Treatment**
  - Refers to intentional discrimination for reasons such as age, race, or gender.
  - You must not use performance appraisals to justify employment decisions really based on discrimination.

- **Disparate (Adverse) Impact**
  - Refers to unintentional discrimination that seem neutral but may adversely impact potential employees because of age, race, gender or other status.
  - Certain performance appraisal practices can operate to exclude certain people from employment opportunities.

- **Civil Rights Act of 1991 (CRA 1991)**
  - Allows plaintiffs to have a jury trial and to receive both compensatory and punitive damages in discrimination cases and alters the burden of proof to make it easier to show bias.
  - Makes it easier to show that practices such as performance appraisal were used to discriminate against an individual or group.

- **Age Discrimination in Employment Act (ADEA)**
  - Prohibits employment discrimination against people 40 years and older.
  - Protects employees from having performance appraisal procedures and results used to continue age-based discrimination.
- **Americans with Disabilities Act 1990 (ADA)**
  - Prohibits discrimination in employment based on disabilities.
  - Limits appraisal criteria to job functions and calls for reasonable accommodation in performance appraisals.

Other Legal Issues

Significant case law has grown up over the years that bears directly on the practice of performance appraisal. Below are some ways in which companies can effectively limit their potential liability based on training, communication, and policy in the context of performance appraisal.

- **Harassment/Constructive Discharge**
  - Make it a requirements that employees notify their manager if issues related to performance or appraisals are so bad that it may cause people to quit their jobs.
  - Set up procedures to investigate and eliminate any such conduct by supervisors or other employees.
- **Age Discrimination**
  - Make sure supervisors receive training to avoid any age-related comments in written and verbal appraisals.
  - Keep performance criteria updated to avoid any potential claim that an older employee was laid off due to lack of new skills.
- **Disability Discrimination**
  - Check appraisal results and recommendations for any evidence that might be perceived as discriminatory.
  - Make sure evaluations cover only essential job functions.

    – Provide training for supervisors to help them identify reasonable accommodations in judging performance and in review procedures.

- **Defamation/Misrepresentation**
  – Set up procedures to make sure no false (either favorable or unfavorable) information appears on performance appraisals.

- **Negligence**
  – Keep employees informed of poor performance so they cannot claim their performance would have improved had they known better.

Final Words of Advice

There are a lot of legal issues in performance appraisal. That is why we present here some cautions from "The Dirty Dozen Performance Appraisal Errors" by Jonathan A. Segal, a partner with the law firm of Duane Morris LLP and managing principal of the Duane Morris Institute (January 14, 2011, *Bloomberg Businessweek*, *www.businessweek.com*).

1. Late Evaluation

Don't procrastinate on performance appraisals. "From an employee relations perspective, the message is clear. You may say in your handbook that you consider employees your most valuable asset, but they now know … it's not true." Being late on appraisals may also hurt your credibility and undermine performance management. How can you criticize your employees for missing deadlines or arriving late for meetings if you set such an example?

2. Overevaluation

Being easy on appraisals "serves as possible evidence of bias (pretext) for legal action" if you later criticize or penalize the employee for performance problems, because the employee might use the appearance of inconsistency as a basis for making a claim of unlawful treatment.

3. Timing Issues

An annual evaluation should cover only that evaluation period.

"Managers should raise prior deficiencies only to the extent they remain, in which event they really are current deficiencies."

4. Inconsistency

Beware of three types of inconsistency:

- Inconsistency between comments and scores on an evaluation
- Inconsistency between the previous year's appraisal and the current appraisal (if the manager has not given notice to the employee when performance started declining)
- Inconsistency in applying standards to employees

5. "Like Me" Bias

This bias, discussed in Chapter 4, "turns into a problem when we focus too much on style or process and not enough on outcome achieved." What matters is whether an employee achieved the desired outcome "in a reasonable way" and not whether he or she did it as the manager would have done.

6. Stereotyping

It may not be obvious, but sometimes stereotyping comes through "in the subtext of comments" in performance appraisals, such as when a manager uses wording such as "lack of commitment" to describe an employee (usually female) who has "primary child- or elder-care responsibilities."

7. Using Labels Rather Than Behaviors

Like stereotyping, you may label a person "lazy" or "unmotivated" rather than providing specific examples of behaviors that represent poor performance of job tasks and responsibilities.

8. Using Absolutes

Extreme comments about an employee being excellent (halo effect) or terrible (horns effect) may not be evidence of discrimination, but it may damage a manager's credibility.

9. Impugning Intent

"Intent is largely irrelevant; you cannot prove it." Making accusations such as "You didn't try" or "You don't care" may seem to an employee like a personal attack. Focus on behavior and results, not intent.

10. Referencing Protected Absences

Take care in mentioning protected leaves (for example, family or medical leave under the Family and Medical Leave Act) when evaluating an employee.

11. One-Sided Dialogue

Always ask your employees their thoughts and feelings about how you've evaluated them—and take their comments seriously.

12. Absence of Goals

Make sure you have set goals and always focus on employee workplace actions and performance.

In summary, what follows a list of actions you can use use as guidance when considering the legal implications of the performance appraisal process:

- Develop an appraisal form that relates specifically to the jobs of your employees.
- Train supervisors and managers in the evaluation process.
- Develop a rating scale that fairly assesses levels of performance.
- Take safeguards against inaccurately rating employee performance.
- Make sure supervisors and managers understand the potential for bias and how to avoid it.
- Consider setting up cross-checks so more than one manager appraises an employee or that managers who know the job responsibilities of the employee check each other's work.
- Managers and employees should agree on the job responsibilities on which employees are evaluated and that they constitute an accurate list of major job duties.
- Employees must sign their appraisals after being given an opportunity to review the evaluation and to provide written comments.
- Set up a procedure for appeal to a higher-level manager for any employee who requests it.

- Set up a schedule for appraisals, including for those who are new and on probation and stick to this schedule.
- Review performance appraisals for any type of discrimination, also known as adverse impact.
- Follow the organization's system or procedures to the letter and refrain from any comments or actions suggesting that continued employment is guaranteed.

7 Following Up After the Performance Appraisal Meeting

W ith this chapter we begin the React stage of the Plan-Do-Check-React performance management cycle presented in Chapter 1. This chapter also finishes the Check stage and begins the Plan stage again—only better.

How the activities discussed in this chapter—diagnosing performance problems, discussing performance improvement, planning for personal development, and setting objectives for the next evaluation period—are handled depends on the organization and the work unit. Some of these activities may be included in the performance appraisal meeting, depending on the performance appraisal procedures at your organization.

These activities are discussed here as forming the agenda for another meeting, for two reasons:

- These matters would generally overload the agenda for the performance appraisal meeting, which may take an hour or longer. To also cover the matters discussed in this chapter would add another hour, maybe more.
- These matters move in different directions, with the emphasis and focus of each being different, as explained in Chapter 4,

where I quoted a human resources consultant who labeled the linking of performance appraisal and personal development "an unholy alliance." Diagnosing performance problems, although naturally a part of discussing the performance appraisal, leads into discussing performance improvement and planning personal development and from there into setting objectives. The discussion of performance is about the past. The discussion of performance improvement, personal development, and new objectives is about the future. These matters should be discussed in an atmosphere that's different from the atmosphere of the performance appraisal meeting.

Now, you may be wondering, "Another meeting?! I've got better things to do than another series of meetings!"

Well, do the math. Or just read how Dick Grote does the math in his book *The Performance Appraisal Question and Answer Book: A Survival Guide for Managers* (AMACOM, 2002).

He calculates the time for the planning meeting (to set objectives) at 45–60 minutes, the time for writing the performance appraisal at 60–90 minutes, and the time for the performance appraisal discussion at 45 minutes. He arrives at a sum of about three hours. To that he adds three hours for "preparation, thinking, and planning," for a total of six hours per employee.

He divides that figure by the standard figure of 2,000 work hours in a year (fifty 40-hour weeks) and arrives at 0.3 percent of a manager's time devoted to "performance management" for each employee. We could quibble about performance management as encompassing more than the three areas of activities that Grote uses in the calculation, but his point stands: *0.3 percent of your time for each employee.*

Whether you schedule the activities discussed in this chapter for a separate meeting or for the performance appraisal meeting or for a series of shorter meetings, what's important is to do them right. And "right" means working with each employee to help that individual develop his or her abilities to work smarter, harder, better, and with greater satisfaction.

Reacting to Good Performance

The first part of the React stage of the performance management cycle is how you respond to the good results your employees have achieved in the performance appraisal in the Check stage. What do your employees deserve for their performance during the past evaluation period?

The ways in which managers react to good performance are often lumped together under the label of "rewards and recognition." Is there a difference between the two? If so, what is that difference—and (why) does it matter?

(I emphasize that rewards and recognition are not appropriate only as a result of the performance appraisal. You should reward and recognize your employees whenever they deserve it. However, the subject seems most logical here, following the performance appraisal meeting, if only because that may be the time when rewards and recognition are most likely in many organizations.)

Reward vs. Recognition

Various ways have been proposed to distinguish between "reward" and "recognition."

Here's a distinction that seems representative of the common conception of the two:

> Recognition has nothing to do with financial rewards. It is about fulfilling psychological needs that we all share—to know that management is aware of and appreciates our contributions and achievements.
>
> Rewards are financial in nature and provide employees with direction to achieve certain outcomes. Financial incentives do not by themselves serve as motivators. They do serve to fulfill employees' desire for monetary gain. They say to employees that we value what you do and want you to share in the rewards of their contributions.
>
> There is a difference between the motivating force of recognition and rewards. Rewards are tangible and work because the employees desire what the organization has to offer in exchange for their

work. Employees know what to expect. This is basically an agreement offering a specific prize for specific performance.

Positive recognition fulfills the employee's need for appreciation. Such appreciation is often accompanied by small gifts, the main value of which is as a symbol and reminder of a job well done.

(Adapted from "Recognition and Rewards: Do You Know the Difference?" by Fritz Edmunds, in *PPB* [*Promotional Products Business*], March 2003)

Other ways to distinguish between the two include:

- Rewards are money or something else that cost the organization and represent a *financial* or *physical* benefit to the employee, while recognition provides a *psychological* benefit.
- Rewards are economic exchanges and extrinsic motivators; recognition is intended to be personally meaningful and touch employees on an emotional level.
- A reward is a thing, something you give, and recognition is an action, something you do.

Do we need to distinguish between rewards and recognition? A more important question: Do *employees* distinguish between reward and recognition? If so, do they distinguish between them in the same ways as employers?

Let's be pragmatic. Whether reward or recognition, the way in which you respond to good performance should generally meet the following criteria:

- The employee must value it.
- It must be affordable.
- It must not be considered an entitlement: if employees expect it, they'll probably appreciate it less and the organization will be committed to providing it.
- It must not promote individual performance to the point of undermining the performance of the team and/or work unit.

Rewards

If you want to give your employees rewards, the sky's the limit—cash bonuses, stock awards/options, and perks like paid parking and gift certificates and car allowances. In actuality, of course, the limit is your budget. There are thousands of sales reps with hundreds of companies who are ready and willing to help you provide any kinds of rewards you may want, so there's no need to list suggestions here.

However, if you don't want to bust your budget on rewards, I can recommend a couple of great resources—

1001 Ways to Reward Employees by Bob Nelson (Workman Publishing, 2nd ed., 2005). Nelson offers enough suggestions that any manager should be able to find some that would work with his or her employees and with any budget.

Recognizing and Rewarding Employees by R. Brayton Bowen (McGraw-Hill, 2000). This provides lots of ideas for how to recognize and reward employee performance and why they work or sometimes don't work.

Recognition

Probably the easiest form of recognition—and also one of the most important to most employees—is *praise*. Yet so many managers neglect this essential of performance management. They get so focused on making sure that their employees are not making mistakes or slacking off that they lose sight of the importance of positive reinforcement.

Keep in mind the wise advice offered by Ken Blanchard in *The One-Minute Manager* (William Morrow, 1982)—"Help people reach their full potential: catch them doing something right." It should not be difficult, but you may have trouble remembering to do it. Bob Nelson and Peter Economy suggest putting the names of your employees on your weekly to-do list and then crossing off the names as you catch your employees doing something right, "in accordance with their performance goals" (*Managing for Dummies*, Wiley Publishing, 2010). If you can't remember the objectives of each of your employees, write up a "cheat sheet." If it seems more natural that you remember the performance problems that you've noted in the appraisal process, then praise them when they're not having those problems. If you catch an employee doing something exceptional, you could follow up on your praise by sending him or her a memo of appreciation (e-mail is fine) and putting a copy in his or her file, so you remember the event when you do performance appraisals.

Consider recognizing employees in ways that involve their jobs, such as the following:

- greater autonomy
- more responsibilities
- more interesting tasks (more enjoyable or more challenging)
- greater authority
- more flexible work schedule
- more travel or less travel
- project assignments
- opportunities for training
- greater input/involvement in decision making

Different Answers

Ask any manager what his or her employees want from their jobs, and you'll probably get a list of items heavy on financial incentives such as increased pay, bonuses, promotions, and so forth. Ask any employee what he or she really wants from his or her job, and you'll likely get a very different answer.

"Yes, salary is important, but even more important are the intangibles of trust and respect, the chance to learn new skills and be involved in decision making, and being thanked for doing good work."

—Bob Nelson and Dean Spitzer, *The 1001 Rewards and Recognition Fieldbook: The Complete Guide* (Workman Publishing, 2003)

According to a survey conducted in 2002 by Bob Nelson, these are the top 10 recognition factors (*The 1001 Rewards and Recognition Fieldbook*):

1. Support and involvement
2. Personal praise
3. Autonomy and authority
4. Flexible working hours

5. Learning and development

6. Manager availability and time

7. Written praise

8. Electronic praise

9. Public praise

10. Cash or cash substitutes

Five Tips

Susan M. Heathfield, a management and organization development consultant specializing in human resources issues, offers the following tips in her article "Five Tips for Effective Employee Recognition":

1. Make all employees eligible for the recognition.
2. Establish criteria for achievements that are worthy of recognition. Then recognize any employee who meets those criteria.
3. Specify the achievement that is being recognized. In other words, don't just say, "We're giving Pete this award because he had a good sales month" or "Antoinette deserves this plaque because she's worked so hard."
4. Give the recognition as soon after the achievement as possible, so you reinforce performance or behaviors you want to encourage.
5. Do not leave it to managers to select the employees to receive recognition. "This type of process will be viewed forever as 'favoritism' or talked about as 'it's your turn to get recognized this month.' This is why processes that single out an individual, such as 'Employee of the Month,' are rarely effective."

Surprise!

According to Heathfield, "People also like recognition that is random and that provides an element of surprise." However, if you recognize every achievement of any type or size with a lunch, for example, gradually that recognition is taken for granted; it becomes an entitlement and loses its impact as recognition.

The Most Important Rule of Rewards and Recognition

There's no shortage of advice out there about rewards and recognition for employees. However, there is one thing that you must always keep in mind, the most important rule of rewards and recognition. It's simply what's known as the Platinum Rule: Treat others as they would like you to treat them.

> **The Platinum Rule**
> "Do unto others as they would like done unto them"—has been proposed
> by Tony Alessandra as "a newer, more sensitive version of the Golden
> Rule." The Golden Rule assumes that all human beings are alike, that what others
> want is the same as what I want. We all know that's just not so. The Platinum Rule
> reminds us to try to respect the "otherness" of other people.

Don't assume. As Anne Bruce puts it in *Building a High-Morale Workplace* (McGraw-Hill, 2003), "Never assume when you can assess." Bruce includes in her book a survey to assess factors that may matter in terms of employee morale. It consists of 18 items that employees are asked to rate on a scale from 1 to 4. You may want to consider developing a similar survey, listing types of rewards and/or recognition for your employees to assess. Don't list anything you're not willing and able to offer your employees. Be as specific as possible. You might also add a few lines so they can add suggestions.

I'd also advise more specifically, "Never assume when you can ask." Bruce offers a very good suggestion, to publicize notable accomplishments of your employees in the organization newsletter and/or the local press. However, what if the employee in question doesn't want the publicity, for whatever reasons? Ask!

Abraham Maslow and Frederick Herzberg

At this point in our discussion of rewards and recognition, we need to consider the work of two psychologists who have helped us better understand what motivates all of us in general and employees in particular. The theories discussed below can help you not only to reward and recognize your employees more appropriately and more effectively, but also to manage performance better.

Abraham Maslow, the renowned psychologist, described human needs in terms of their importance. He established five levels in his hierarchy of needs (Exhibit 7-1).

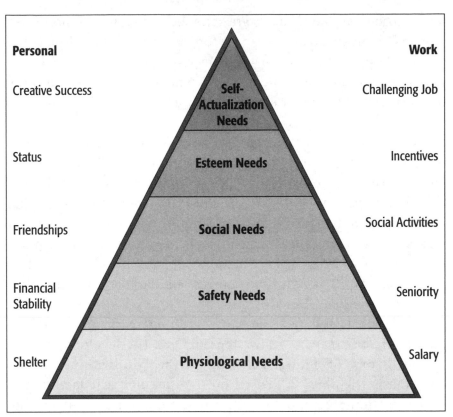

Exhibit 7-1. Hierarchy of Needs

- *Physiological* needs (such as breathing, water, food, sleep, sex, and shelter)
- *Safety* needs (security of body, of health, of resources, of property, of employment, of family, of morality)
- *Social* needs (e.g., friendship, love, family, sexual intimacy)
- *Esteem* needs (such as self-esteem, confidence, achievement, respect for others)
- *Self-actualization* needs (e.g., morality, spontaneity, creativity, and problem-solving).

So, here is what we learn from the hierarchy of needs that applies to our discussion of rewards and recognition. The lower levels—physiological needs and social needs—are basic. We are motivated to satisfy those needs first and foremost. However, once those lower-level needs are satisfied, when we are no longer worried about survival, we are no longer motivated by things that would simply satisfy lower-level needs. In other words, when a person is operating at a higher level where esteem needs are the primary motivator, he or she is most interested in things that satisfy those higher needs.

In most work situations, a pay increase of a few percent will not have much power to motivate an employee. (Since the satisfaction of our lower-level needs is a question of real and emotional security, it will be affected by such things as job uncertainty, a bad economy, or sudden financial or material losses.) What matters are those intrinsic rewards that can help satisfy our higher-level needs, such as recognition, the respect of others, accomplishments, and self-respect. So that's an important lesson we can learn from Maslow.

Frederick Herzberg, a researcher doing work in the 1960s, took motivation theory a few steps further. He developed a two-factor theory of motivation called the Motivation-Hygiene Hypothesis (Exhibit 7-2), based on the idea that satisfaction and dissatisfaction are not on a continuum, but are independent phenomena.

He said that there were factors that drove motivation, which he called, simply enough, "satisfiers." They include achievement, recognition, the work itself, responsibility, advancement, and growth, in that order. With satisfiers, the more the better: the more these motivators played a part in work, the better people felt about their jobs and the more rewarded they felt.

He said that there were also factors that operated as "dissatisfiers," which he called "hygiene factors." (He used this term because his original work was done in hospitals, where hygiene is commonly used and understood.) The hygiene factors include company policies, supervision, relationship with supervisors, salary, relationship with peers, personal life, relationship with subordinates, status, and security. Hygiene factors affect motivation more by their absence than by their presence. That's why

Herzberg called them *dissatisfiers*. They operate like Maslow's lower-level motivators: you need them, but once you have them they cease to motivate.

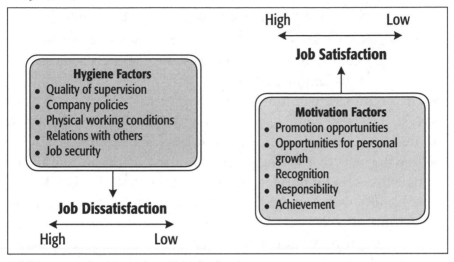

Exhibit 7-2. Motivation-Hygiene Hypothesis

The lesson for managers here is twofold:

1. Do what it takes to eliminate the negative effect of dissatisfiers.
2. Take action to increase the positive effects of satisfiers.

What can managers do to reduce the effects of "dissatisfiers"?

- Be aware of potentially controversial company policy decisions and help employees understand and accept them.
- Be sensitive to your relationships with your employees and act to diffuse any possible conflict before it becomes problematic.
- Keep employees informed of company developments that may affect them.
- Know your employees; be sensitive to any feelings about their work and the workplace that may be affecting them negatively.
- Keep tabs on issues that may get in the way of work, such as break time, temperature, and availability of supplies and resources.

- Know what's going on between and among your employees and among team members, and do what you can to maintain morale and diffuse problems before they become serious.

What can managers do to increase the effects of "satisfiers"?

- Manage by walking around: your presence shows an interest in your employees—and the interest of the boss is seen as positive by most employees.
- Give public recognition to your employees.
- Listen to what employees say about improving their work and give them the responsibility for taking on new things.
- Use the objective-setting process to identify for each employee objectives that represent significant achievements; let the others know when an employee has achieved one of his or her significant objectives.
- Give employees the chance to stretch in setting their objectives. Have at least one that may be beyond them, but reward them for their efforts to achieve it.
- Always have at least one personal growth objective for every employee and monitor it during the course of the year.

Pay for Performance

In discussions of rewards and recognition, a subject that comes up frequently is pay for performance. It would seem very natural to pay employees for performance that contributes to a healthier bottom line.

Yes, it seems logical and sensible to link pay with performance, but there are problems.

Putting money on the table makes any differences of perspective and opinion over appraisals even more difficult and makes disagreement more likely and more serious. Pay for performance tends to make managers and employees adversaries, which makes it harder for them to work together to discuss and solve performance problems.

Tying money to appraisals makes it even more important for them to be accurate, precise, valid, and completely fair—an impossibility. Also, the appraisals might be more in danger of legal challenges because of the money involved.

Finally, money makes employees more individualistic and less interested in working for the success of their team and their work unit. The money at stake makes it more probable that employees who work closely together will blame each other for problems that may jeopardize their individual chances to earn the pay for performance prize.

According to Robert Bacal, author of *Performance Management* (McGraw-Hill, 1999), the best way to link pay to performance is to make it part of the performance planning process, by establishing the criteria for pay increases when you are setting objectives and standards for the evaluation period. Don't tie pay to ratings or rankings, Bacal warns. Make the criteria as measurable as possible, as objective as possible, to reduce the chance of arguments.

In *The Performance Appraisal Handbook: Legal and Practical Rules for Managers* (Nolo, 2nd ed., 2007), Amy DelPo makes an important point:

> Some managers may have a gut feeling about who should get a raise—a feeling often based on soft factors such as whom they like and whom they relate to best. Linking a raise to a performance review can be risky because a manager may—consciously or not—write the appraisal to support a raise decision, rather than base the decision on the appraisal. In such cases, neither the salary decisions nor the reviews make much sense. And if a lawsuit arises, the appraisal may not adequately explain why a certain employee got a raise but another did not.

The key, Bacal stresses, is to think of your job as helping each of your employees achieve those objectives and earn that pay for performance. He suggests learning about alternative ways to reward good performance and to consider using several ways rather than one single way.

Performance Diagnosis

As mentioned in Chapter 5, performance diagnosis often begins during the performance appraisal meeting. However, as also mentioned there, you should resist the slippery slope from performance review into performance diagnosis. Now is the time to finish the discussion of the reasons for performance problems, making a transition from the Check stage of the performance management cycle into the React stage.

Performance diagnosis is the process we use to determine the factors that are causing an employee to perform in a specific way, whether below standards or expectations or very well. It's basically problem solving, but it requires managers to be sensitive and use tact as they're using problem-solving tools.

> **Performance diagnosis** is the process we use to determine the factors causing an employee to perform in a specific way, whether below standards or expectations or very well.

Begin by choosing one of the performance problems that you mentioned during the appraisal meeting. State the problem as you did during the meeting. Give the examples that you presented at that time. Also mention the extent of the impact of this problem. Employees tend to take their performance problems more seriously when they are aware of how they affect coworkers, for example, or the financial situation in the work unit.

An employee with performance problems can cause problems for other employees in the work unit. They may be forced to work more to compensate for the poor performer; as a result, they're likely to feel frustrated and to resent both the employee and you. The frustration and resentment can flare up as anger and hostility and it can also cause negativity and apathy, affecting even your good employees. Sometimes employees may not be aware of their impact, so it's important to make that clear. (Sometimes employees may not care about their impact. That can cause a performance problem for *you*.)

If you can't make a strong case for the impact of the problem, maybe it's not worth the effort to diagnose and try to solve—at least not yet. You've got to be able to prioritize the problems and choose the most serious to discuss.

(It may make sense with some employees to stagger the performance diagnosis process. You could, for example, focus on the four worst problems at this meeting and then maybe several months later, if you feel that your employee has been improving satisfactorily in those areas, the two of you could meet to discuss the next problems on your list.)

Give Them All Attention

Too often managers may spend far more time focusing on employees who aren't meeting expectations than on employees who are performing well. While it's necessary to try to help the employees with problems perform better, you shouldn't neglect the others.

Even your best workers can be better. Make sure you pay attention to them and provide guidance so they can develop their full potential. That's just a smart use of your "human assets"—and you may be helping those good employees continue to be interested and motivated ... and continue working with you. (It would be a shame if good employees developed attitude problems or left to work elsewhere in hopes of receiving more attention and appreciation.)

Invest sufficient time and effort in your good and better employees during the performance appraisal process. Then, throughout the evaluation period, remember to show that you appreciate them and provide the support to help them do even better.

Approaches and Tools

The most effective approach to diagnosing performance difficulties is using questions. In Chapters 4 and 5 we discussed the use of closed questions, open questions, directional questions, and high-gain questions during the performance appraisal meeting. In performance diagnosis, you continue with your employee the discussion you started during that meeting.

Closed questions—those intended to elicit an answer of "Yes" or "No"—aren't likely to be very effective, except possibly to get the conversation started. However, if you ask questions that require minimal participation—"Yes," "No," nod the head, shake the head, shrug the shoulders—you may be setting up a one-sided discussion, which is definitely not what you want to do.

Directional questions—those that present two or more options and call for a choice—are more effective, but best used to follow up on responses. You may find a need to use a few directional questions if you're having trouble engaging your employee, since they force a choice. (Of course, if the employee is reluctant to participate in the discussion or if you've started with closed questions, he or she may respond to your directional questions with "I don't know" or even shrugging.)

Open questions—because they place no explicit restrictions on the answer—are better for engaging your employee to participate more actively in discussing his or her performance problems.

One of the tools often used in problem solving is *brainstorming.* Robert Bacal suggests it for performance diagnosis meetings as a way to generate thinking and discussion (*Performance Improvement*). But this type of brainstorming would involve only two people, not a team, and you would not be following the usual rules as with group use. You would first determine the basis facts of the performance (when it happened, how frequently, and in what circumstances), facts that you likely presented to your employee during the performance appraisal meeting. Then Bacal recommends beginning like this: "Let's see how many possible causes of this problem we can come up with. We'll just blurt them out, make a quick note, and not discuss them. Then we'll go back and see what makes sense." This approach is casual and the brainstorming should just flow. In a way, this two-person brainstorming is like an extended open question.

Another standard problem-solving tool you should consider in performance diagnosis is the *Five Whys.* This is a simple technique used to explore cause-and-effect relationships underlying a particular problem, with the goal being to determine a root cause. This technique consists of asking "Why" questions to probe into a problem and follow cause-and-effect chains.

> **Five Whys**
> This is a standard problem-solving tool used to explore cause-and-effect relationships underlying a particular problem, with the goal being to determine a root cause. It consists simply of asking "Why" questions to probe into a problem and follow cause-and-effect chains.

Here's an example:

Manager: "You've turned in three important reports after the specified deadline. Why?"

Employee: "I guess it's because I don't write very well, so it takes me longer."

Manager: "Why don't you write very well?"

Employee: "Mostly because I start writing and then I have to rearrange what I've written and I forget to mention things."

Manager: "Why do you have to rearrange what you've written and forget to mention things?"

Employee: "I don't know. Probably because I'm not very organized when I write longer things, like reports."

Manager: "Why are you not very organized when you write longer things?"

Employee: "When I start writing, I think I know what I want to say—it's all in my head, you know. But then ..."

Manager: "Why do you start writing when you have what you want to say in your head?"

Employee: "Oh, you mean like instead of writing out some notes first?"

And then the manager might suggest that the employee try organizing by making an outline before starting to write.

Most of the examples of the Five Whys technique suggest that dialogues between manager and employee are more structured, almost mechanical. However, that doesn't seem realistic. Don't expect to just ask, "Why?" five times. Don't expect your employee to give simple, straightforward answers that you can easily make into "Why?" questions. You'll probably need to paraphrase. Also, sometimes an answer can suggest more than one direction to pursue. Here in our example, when the employee answers, "Mostly because I start writing and then I have to rearrange what I've written and I forget to mention things," the manager could take this as two answers, rather than a combined answer, and pursue either part of the answer, to arrive at a suggestion like mind-mapping to deal with the forgetting problem, and then recommend outlining to deal with the organizing problem.

Performance diagnosis is generally not so complex a problem-solving experience as to warrant using a *cause-and-effect diagram* (aka *Ishikawa diagram* or *fishbone diagram*). However, if you find that your questions and the employee's answers are leading you to explore more than one cause for the performance difficulties, it may be worthwhile to use a cause-and-effect diagram. But don't sketch it out in full from the start, drawing the bone structure and marking the major categories of possible causes as users do when considering the conventional categories of People, Methods, Machines, Materials, Measurements, Environment. Instead, tag the bones as you realize the need to explore a category of possible causes.

Causes and Possible Solutions

The causes of performance problems fall into a few categories. You may want to analyze your employee's problems in terms of the following categories. For each category but the last, there are a few questions listed. I hope they raise issues that you should consider as possible causes for performance problems. There are also some possibilities for remedying the problems. You should always ask your employee to propose possible solutions: "What could you do to improve this situation?"

Expectations

- Does your employee know exactly what's expected of him or her?
- Does your employee know the goals and the outcomes you expect?
- Do you find your employee engaged in activities that aren't part of his or her responsibilities, such as helping other employees with their tasks?

Sometimes employees are not actually aware of a problem with their performance until the manager points it out during the appraisal meeting. If your employee hasn't understood your expectations, there are several things you can do.

If he or she is unclear on the responsibilities, clarify them and explain why your employee must fulfill those responsibilities. It may also help to explain the role of your employee in terms of connections in a network. What do other employees expect him or her to provide them?

If your employee is confused about the extent of his or her responsibilities and authority (boundary issues), you can explain the responsibilities of employees just outside his or her boundaries, to better demarcate the borderlines.

If your employee doesn't understand certain job tasks or procedures, clarify and make sure he or she has written procedures and/or instructions. Depending on the situation, you might ask him or her to talk you through the task or procedure. When you determine the specific areas causing the difficulties, you can explain what your employee needs to understand. Then make a point of providing frequent feedback on those aspects of the task and your expectations.

Resources

- Does your employee have the necessary resources to do his or her job?
- If your employee wants to check with you about some aspect of the job or discuss something with you, are you available?

- Do you occasionally see your employee walking by your office door and glancing at you?

Ask your employee questions that will get the answers to these and other, more specific questions about whatever resources he or she needs. Don't ask, for example, "Do you have all the resources you need?" You're likely to get the easiest answer— "Yes." Ask, "What resources do you sometimes need and not have?" or "What things would help enable you to do your job properly all the time?" In addition to the more obvious resources, your employee may need ready access to information. Not knowing what we need to know and being uncertain can cause us to do our jobs more slowly, to question ourselves, and to delay.

Make a point to ensure that he or she gets the resources needed. Getting answers about the resources your employee needs should be easy—unless the resource that's lacking is *you*. If your employee feels uncomfortable being frank with you, then that's another problem you should tackle. You could start by asking, "How often do you feel a need to ask me about something?"

System

- Do you sometimes forget to promote good two-way communication with your employees?
- Do you assign your employees to team projects without checking their schedules and workloads?
- Are you sometimes negligent about scheduling assignments and deadlines appropriately?
- Do you make a point of praising your employees when they do well?
- Does it seem that at times you're just finding examples of poor performance and few, if any, examples of good work?
- Do your employees ever complain that their project teams have too few people?

Sometimes work culture and peer pressure make it difficult to work efficiently or care about the job. Sometimes managers assign tasks that decrease attention to regular job responsibilities.

Sometimes good performance is not rewarded appropriately and poor performance is tolerated.

Your employee may not be willing or able to answer your questions about difficulties caused by you or his or her coworkers. Probe but don't pressure. If you seem open to explanations and willing to help, your employee should respond, with time.

Abilities

- Does your employee have the abilities to do his or her job?
- Do you ever find your employee asking coworkers how to do tasks?
- Does it ever happen that coworkers will be helping your employee with tasks or even doing tasks for him or her?
- Does your employee get overwhelmed by his or her work?
- Does your employee manage his or her tasks and time effectively?

When we talk about "abilities," what do we mean? Do we mean "aptitudes" or "skills"?

Aptitudes are innate talents or strengths that give a person the capacity to learn. A person with a poor aptitude for a task could never learn how to do it well, even with training and experience.

Skills are what we have when we start with aptitudes and then apply learning, training, and experience.

If you determine that your employee lacks the appropriate skills, then you should provide the training that will enable your employee to develop the necessary skills—either formal training or on-the-job training. You could also coach your employee and/or team him or her with a coworker for peer mentoring.

If it's a question of aptitude, you've got a square peg in a round hole. You may be able to reassign your employee to a suitable job. If that's not possible, you may not have any practical option but to terminate him or her.

Motivation

- Does your employee seem cynical about things in the workplace?

- Does your employee often criticize or complain?
- Does it seem that your employee gets angry easily?
- Does your employee express concerns about tasks that you don't consider really difficult?
- Does it seem that your employee lacks enthusiasm when starting a project?

Sometimes it's easy to recognize a bad attitude or poor morale or low confidence. On the other hand, it may be expressed in less obvious ways.

- Is your employee absent a lot or frequently arriving late?
- Does your employee avoid participating in meetings?
- Is your employee slow to start tasks and/or to finish them?
- Does your employee procrastinate on tasks?
- Does it seem like your employee acts as if overwhelmed by tasks?

If a bad attitude, poor morale, or low self-confidence is causing or contributing to your employee's performance problem, try to determine the underlying cause(s). (We discuss motivation in Chapter 8.) A motivation problem could result from confusion over expectations. A motivation problem may be the result of being unable to do the job right. (How many of us feel motivated to do a task that makes us feel inadequate or stupid?) Then you should determine the cause of the inability, whether it's a lack of resources, lack of training, lack of experience, or lack of aptitude. A motivation problem could be caused by a lack of self-confidence. Your employee may need more reassurance and guidance from you.

Find out what matters to that employee. Anne Bruce advises, "Never assume when you can assess," and she suggests giving employees an assessment tool, which she calls "What Matters to You?" (*Building a High-Morale Workplace*). Employees are asked to rank from 1 to 4 the 18 items listed on the tool in terms of importance to their motivation:

1. My manager showing care and concern for me as a person

2. Good working relationship with my manager

3. Feeling empowered

4. Manager's ability to make decisions

5. Manager who walks the talk

6. Recognition of my efforts

7. Delegation of responsibility to me

8. Being promoted

9. Customer contact

10. Compensation

11. Getting along with others

12. Honest praise

13. Helpful and corrective feedback

14. Coaching

15. The result of a job well done

16. Attending social functions with team members

17. Being given clear objectives

18. Job security

These are suggestions, of course; notice that they cover the map. You may want to ask how they feel about other items. Their responses will probably surprise you. Once you know what matters most and least to each of your employees, you can motivate them as individuals.

Personal Issues

There may be something happening in your employee's life that is affecting him or her at work.

It can be difficult to separate work performance problems from personal problems. But you must avoid any personal issues and focus only on performance issues. Even if you are sure you know what those personal issues are, don't let them enter into your performance diagnosis.

You may feel tempted to help your employee by discussing his or her personal problems. Don't do it. This is a form of enabling. If you try to help, you make it less likely that your employee will take action to deal with those issues appropriately.

That's his or her responsibility. (Your organization may have some form of employee assistance program. If so, it's safest to say only something like "If you have personal problems that are affecting your work, remember that we have an employee assistance program.")

"The System"

Notice that our analysis of performance problems begins with how you and "the system" may have contributed to the employee's performance problem. You should be open to the possibility, perhaps even the *probability*, that the problem is the result of *system* factors more than of *individual* factors.

System factors are "causes of success and failure that are beyond the control of individual employees," such as "poor workflow, excessive bureaucracy, poor communication, and inadequate tools and equipment," while *individual* factors are "characteristics of the employee that *we* believe determine success," such as "motivation level, commitment, skill, knowledge, dexterity, and ability to think" (Robert Bacal, *Performance Management*, emphasis added).

W. Edwards Deming, the efficiency expert credited for the origin of Total Quality Management, listed as one of the "seven deadly diseases" (*Out of the Crisis*, MIT Press, 2000) "Evaluation of performance, merit rating, or annual review." And in "a lesser category of obstacles" he included placing blame on workers, who are "only responsible for 15 percent of mistakes" while "the system desired by management is responsible for 85 percent of the unintended consequences."

It makes sense in terms of the probabilities to start the diagnosis by examining system factors. It makes sense also in terms of your employee's feelings not to begin with individual factors, which could feel like you're starting by blaming him or her.

Bacal makes two interesting points to keep in mind. The first is that "even problems that ... seem a result of flaws in the individual may be caused by the system." He offers as an example a conflict between two employees because they understand their areas of responsibility differently. The second point: "Don't assume that a performance gap is caused by individual factors just because it occurs with just one person doing the job, and not with other people doing the same job." People in the same circumstances won't necessarily react in the same way. So, he adds, if you find the problem lies in the system and you fix that problem, you will improve the performance in question and possibly the performance of other employees doing that job.

What Kind of Manager Are You?

In an influential book published in 1960, *The Human Side of Enterprise*, Douglas McGregor proposed an approach to understanding management in terms of two theories about how managers see human nature—Theory X and Theory Y.

Theory X managers believe that people are innately lazy, that they don't want to work and they don't want greater responsibility. As a result, managers must be very involved in supervising their employees.

Theory Y managers believe that most people may be self-motivated and may enjoy working, performing well, and assuming additional responsibilities. Theory Y managers think of their role in terms of guiding employees toward achieving their potential.

McGregor based his work on Maslow's hierarchy of needs (discussed earlier in this chapter) and suggested that managers could motivate their employees by using either "lower-order" needs (Theory X) or "higher-order" needs (Theory Y).

Theory Y Thinking

The six beliefs or assumptions that we quoted in Chapter 1 are an excellent example of Theory Y thinking, particularly this one: "Most employees, once they understand what's required of them, will make every effort to meet those requirements."

Diagnosing Success

In defining performance diagnosis, we said that it's a process for determining the factors causing an employee to perform in a specific way, whether below standards or expectations or *very well*.

Managers generally focus on performance below standards or expectations and don't try to diagnose "success stories." We may praise and celebrate good performance, we may hold up excellent employees as models for others to emulate, but how often do we seriously try to figure out why some employees perform so well?

Some Models Don't Work

Managers will sometimes (often?) try to motivate their employees by holding up the best employee as a model—"Most of you have been making far too many data entry mistakes lately. Tanina hardly ever makes a mistake. Why can't the rest of you be more like her?"

That's a bad way to try to motivate employees. It's likely to just motivate them to resent the model employee or be jealous or annoyed with you.

You can discuss and analyze good performance in much the same way as you discuss and analyze poor performance. Ask "How?" questions like "How were you able to get all of your monthly reports to me on time or even early this year?" or "How did you produce widgets that were 97 percent up to specs in the third quarter?" Notice that these example questions focus on specific achievements for a specific time. The more specific you can be with your questions, the easier it should be for your employee to be specific about the "success factors." Follow up on the answers that suggest a factor you could share with your other employees.

Sharing Time

How do you share the "secrets of success"? Hold a big meeting after you finish all of the individual meetings. Instead of focusing on the performance problems, as managers tend to feel responsible for doing, focus on the success factors. And do it without naming names. For example, "I'd like to share with you some ideas that may help you do your jobs better. Those of you who are doing data entry could try ... You people inspecting widgets might want to try ..."

Serious Attitude Problems

Sometimes the attempt to diagnose a general performance problem reveals an attitude problem. You should try to determine the cause of this problem, of course. However, talking about it with your employee may give you the feeling that there's no specific cause. The problem may be what some people would label as "intentional poor performance" or even as "willful misconduct." An employee may simply not care about doing his or her best and you may doubt that he or she would respond well to a change in job tasks, responsibilities, or situation.

You could decide that the best remedy would be to give your employee a warning or an official reprimand. Unfortunately, a warning may be just an unpleasant moment for the employee, with no effect on his or her performance, and putting a reprimand in his or her file may not affect him or her at all.

Verbal warnings and written reprimands are only a part of a *progressive discipline process,* which may consist of the following:

- oral warning
- formal oral warning with documentation
- written warning
- final warning
- termination

(This is just an example. You should know and use the specific process established by your human resources office.) If the disciplinary actions don't go beyond warnings and reprimands, you may actually be encouraging poor performance. So, when you are trying to determine why an employee isn't doing as well as you expect, the reason may be that there is no real negative consequence for employees who perform poorly.

Progressive Discipline
A progressive discipline process is a program for dealing with employee problems through activities intended to modify behavior by applying a series of increasingly severe punishments for unacceptable behavior.

Managers may think in terms of black and white—either terminate the employee or keep giving warnings and reprimands. Here are some negative consequences to try if you believe that an employee is choosing not to meet expectations:

- Check on the employee more frequently. That's a simple negative consequence, since employees who are not performing up to their abilities don't like having the boss around as a witness. Your presence may be one of the most powerful management interventions for improving performance.
- Assign the employee to tasks and/or work conditions that he or she will like less than the current tasks and/or conditions.
- Restrict privileges the employee enjoys, such as flexibility of schedule.
- Deny pay raises until the employee's performance improves.
- Demote the employee—and reduce his or her salary.

If the negative consequences you apply lead to an improvement in performance, encourage the employee to maintain the improvement with a positive consequence. If not, then your only choice may be termination.

Why try to help a problem employee? Why not start procedures to terminate? There are at least six good reasons to make the effort.

1. The performance problem could be the result of a square peg in a round hole. If the employee is in a job that's not right for his or her skills and/or personality, a change in responsibilities could resolve the problem.
2. You don't want to convey the message to your other employees that performance problems can easily mean termination.
3. Your work unit won't be healthier or more productive if your employees are afraid.
4. It often is less expensive to help a problem employee improve than to recruit, hire, and train someone to replace that employee.
5. If you terminate an employee without making a good effort to help him or her and then follow the standard termination process, you could risk some legal difficulties.
6. The problem employee's behavior may be the result of a bigger or more pervasive problem in your work unit—conflicts with other employees, a difficult work environment, cultural

differences? Consider all factors that could contribute to the problem, including your perception of the employee and any bias in your appraisal of him or her.

Continuous Performance Diagnosis

The process presented here for diagnosing performance problems (or, at least in principle, performance successes) is not only good for following up on the performance appraisal meeting. Use this process any time during the evaluation period. It can be appropriate for any occasion when you and an employee discuss his or her performance.

Performance Improvement Planning

When you and your employee develop a performance improvement plan, you are shifting from the React stage of the performance management cycle to the Plan stage.

A performance improvement plan is the documentation of performance expectations that manager and employee develop together to outline the actions that both will take to remedy specified performance problems. We suggest you and your employee draft the plan together. Ask him or her for suggestions. Your employee will be responsible for the success of the plan, so involve him or her in developing it.

For each performance problem that you decide to include in the plan:

- Describe the tasks your employee is not performing at an acceptable level. If you wrote a narrative for this problem on your appraisal form, you may choose to use that, although you may want to revise it based on your discussion of the problem with your employee.
- Set objectives that are SMART (described in Chapter 2).
- Specify the time frame within which you expect your employee to achieve the objective.
- Schedule interim checkpoints for meeting with your employee to assess his or her progress toward that objective.

- Specify any training you require and provide for your employee. This depends, of course, on the factors you've identified as contributing to the performance problem, especially if the problem was caused by a deficiency in abilities.
- State how you will help and support your employee. Your role in the improvement effort will depend on the factors identified as contributing to the performance problem, especially if the problem was caused by system factors, difficulty understanding expectations, a lack of resources, or motivation.
- State the positive outcomes of completing the plan successfully. Don't put something like "You get to keep your job." You might promise to put a document in his or her personnel file stating he or she has remedied the specified performance deficiencies.
- State the negative consequences of not meeting the specified performance criteria. (If these consequences include progressive discipline, follow whatever process and guidelines your human resources office has established.)
- Ask your employee to read, date, and sign the plan, to acknowledge that he or she has read the plan and understands what it requires.

You may want to call your performance improvement plan (PIP) by another name. It seems that a PIP is generally considered a prelude to a pink slip. As Alan L. Slover, employment attorney and strategist for 30 years, once commented in his online forum, "Whenever a client or blog reader tells me he or she has been placed on a so-called Performance Improvement Plan, or PIP, I worry for them. In over 25 years of counseling and representing employees, I

A ***performance improvement plan*** is the documentation of performance expectations that manager and employee develop together to outline the actions that both will take to remedy specified performance problems. It should specify the standards by which the employee's improvement will be evaluated and set a date for the manager and the employee to meet to discuss the status of the improvement project.

can count on one hand the number who have remained employed at the conclusion of a PIP ... unless they've stood up for themselves by challenging the PIP." Of course, if you work out a performance improvement plan with all of your employees, they are much less likely to take it as the beginning of the end.

> **Be Purposeful**
> If you need to lay out a performance improvement plan, do it with the purpose of helping your employee improve, not the purpose of satisfying a requirement in the progressive discipline process. This is easier to do if you draft the plan with your employee.

We conclude this discussion of performance improvement plans with these basics:

- Define the problem. Specify the tasks, responsibilities, or behaviors.
- Define the improvement required. What must your employee do?
- Set the standards you will use for appraising the results of your employee's efforts.
- Establish short-range and long-range goals and timetables.
- Specify actions you require of your employee, such as training.
- Specify how you will help.
- State the consequences, both positive and negative.

Performance Planning

The next part of the planning process is to set performance objectives. Since Chapter 2 focused on setting objectives, there's only one thing to emphasize here: *involve your employee.*

We involved the employees in setting objectives in Chapter 2, of course. However, after discussing their appraisal with you and diagnosing their performance with you, they should be able to take a more active role in the process. If they are more involved in establishing criteria by which you will evaluate them, they may feel more responsible for succeeding and less like the criteria are something you've imposed on them.

Now that you and your employee have communicated about his or her performance in the appraisal discussion and worked together to identify problems and weaknesses in the diagnosis discussion, you should be better able to use what you've learned to plan better, to raise the level of the Plan stage of the cycle this time around. In the same way, your actions during the Do stage of the cycle (which we discuss in Chapter 8) will enable both of you to move to a higher level of the Check stage this next time through the cycle. And what you will be doing better in the Check stage should enable you to improve the resulting React and Plan stages. As a result, the performance management cycle should continue spiraling upward.

You and your employee may decide that you should meet during the year, maybe every three or four months, so you can discuss any issues and make course corrections to keep the employee on track. (This also could help your employees be more attentive to documenting their achievements.) You may also decide, based on your discussion about his or her performance, that your employee could benefit from special attention, maybe some coaching or mentoring. This is not about solving problems, but about improving performance that's already acceptable.

By the end of the performance planning process, Bacal states in *Performance Management*, you and each employee should be able to answer a series of questions in the same way, including questions like:

- Which of the employee's job responsibilities are most important?
- Which of the employee's job responsibilities are least important?
- How will the manager and the employee know at any point how well the employee is doing his or her job?
- What level of authority does the employee have to do his or her job tasks?
- How do the employee's job responsibilities contribute to the work unit and the organization?
- How can the manager help the employee do his or her job tasks better, more efficiently, and/or more easily?

- How will the manager and the employee communicate about job tasks to prevent problems and keep current on the employee's performance?
- How will the manager and the employee work to resolve any difficulties the employee encounters in doing his or her job?
- Does the employee need to develop any new skills or abilities to do the job?

Improve Job Descriptions

You and your employee may decide at this point that his or her job description should be revised and updated. (It could be that your human resources office requires you to do so annually. If so, that's great!) The responsibilities may have changed or the priorities of the tasks may have shifted. Never allow your job descriptions to get dusty or rusty.

Job descriptions should not only be accurate but also complete. That includes specifying responsibilities and authority.

Job Descriptions for All

Here's an interesting suggestion: "Publish all the job descriptions so everyone can see them. That way, not only will people know what to do, they will know what not to do and what to expect from others" ("Are We Afraid to Tackle Poor Performers?" Les Potton, freelance people management consultant, Target HR).

Personal Development Planning

This planning is all about your employee's personal agenda of career development, job satisfaction, and future growth. The employee should take the lead here.

(In some organizations, performance improvement planning is only for the worst employees and the others get personal development planning, with the purpose of helping them do their jobs even better. That's really not *personal* development, just *individual*. Here, we're taking personal development as being guided by personal interests.)

The standard question for starting a discussion of personal

development is "What do you want to be doing X years from now?" That question can be overwhelming for some employees—especially those who have just been through a difficult performance appraisal and diagnosis process. You might adjust the time period in terms of your employee's job performance and personality factors, such as self-confidence, ambition, and motivation.

Your employees may not all want to answer truthfully, particularly those who hope to leave your organization and don't want you to help them leave earlier than they plan. If your employee hesitates to respond, you might shorten the timeframe—without speculating on the reason for the hesitation.

Again, this is all about what your employee wants. This is about his or her future, whether your employee is willing and able to talk about 5 or 10 years down the road or only the next 6 months.

Then, ask how you can help. Your employee may not be able to answer that question, at least on the spot. If you get an answer, determine how you can provide the help needed. If not, invite your employee to think about it and come talk with you whenever he or she has some ideas. Don't try to be helpful by suggesting possibilities. Your employee might take your suggestions as things that *you* want, not things that *he* or *she* might want.

You can do personal development planning more formally, in a separate meeting with preparation. (Of course, if your organization has specific processes and procedures, that's what you do.) In many or most cases, that would mean more time and effort for you—and more pressure on your employees.

Should you write up the results of personal development planning? Maybe as you'd write up the minutes of a meeting, along these lines: "[Employee] expressed interest in doing ..." "[Manager] agreed to help by ..." You and your employee could sign the document to acknowledge that these minutes fairly represent the substance of your meeting.

> **PA and Career Development Are Separate**
> You should not confuse career development and performance appraisal or discuss both during a performance review meeting. While career development may come in such meetings, it is not a good idea when the purpose of meeting affects the employee's salary. It's a common practice in many companies to discuss career opportunities at six-month intervals between annual review meetings. In that way you keep performance appraisals focused on current job responsibilities and career development meetings focused on ways employees can move forward in the organization.

Performance Appraisal Responsibilities of Your Employees

As stressed throughout this chapter, the performance appraisal process should be collaborative. After setting the objectives for the coming evaluation period, close by making sure that your employee is aware of his or her ongoing responsibilities in that process.

It may be smart to give each employee a list of those responsibilities that he or she can keep to serve as a reminder. Here is a generic example.

- Throughout the year, keep a log of your accomplishments or outstanding performance (for example, projects you've completed, workshops you've attended or given, new programs you've developed and implemented, commendations you've received, etc.).
- If you are assigned any tasks or responsibilities not on your job description, document them (tasks or responsibility, date assigned, circumstances, other relevant information) so you can discuss revising your job description with your manager.
- Take note of ideas you have about areas for improvement or development. Be sure to mention these when you meet with your manager as scheduled.

Closure and Overture

At this point we end the Check and React and Plan stages of the performance management cycle and we devote the following chapter to the Do stage.

8 Performance Management as a Continuous Process

The Do stage of the performance management cycle consists entirely of … managing performance. To be more accurate, it's actually about making better performance possible.

Most of the performance management activities discussed in this chapter are done simultaneously throughout the time between performance appraisals and planning sessions.

Schedule Your Commitments

First, schedule your commitments. In the performance diagnosis and planning meeting, you committed to meeting with each of your employees, so you should put those meetings on your calendar.

I'll repeat here a point made in Chapter 4 about the performance appraisal meeting: take the scheduled meetings seriously. Don't bump meetings you've scheduled with your employees when other things come up. Doing so sends the message that you're not serious about helping your employees do their jobs better, that it's not a high priority. How does that affect their motivation to improve? How does that affect their trust in you to walk the talk?

Consider the commitment you make when meeting with each of your employees to be the *minimum* responsibility you're assuming with him or her. That, in a way, is your performance objective. Each of your employees is most likely going to be mentally appraising you by how well you do as you've promised him or her.

(Of course, your employees won't be doing official, written appraisals of your performance—or, if you or your organization provides them with that opportunity, they probably won't be commenting on instances when you've failed to fulfill your commitments to them. But the results of their mental appraisals of you, their feelings about any failure to keep your word, are naturally going to affect their motivation to work harder, smarter, and more effectively and efficiently. So, in a way, that's performance management—but in the wrong direction.)

You should also make other promises—to provide training, resources, etc.—part of your schedule. You may choose to schedule reminders or you may simply want to post reminder notes on your wall—whatever works for you.

Continue the Process of Diagnosis and Improvement

Analyzing and taking action to fix problems should not be something you do only around the yearly performance appraisals. According to Robert Bacal in *Performance Management*, "There is a mistaken idea that the only way performance gaps or deficits are identified is during the yearly performance appraisal meetings. That's dangerous thinking." He asserts that managers should identify problems at all times in three ways:

1. Through information they collect continuously about the key functions of the organization
2. Through regular communication with their employees
3. Through paying attention—the old management-by-walking-around approach

We discuss the second and third ways in this chapter.

Coaching Your Employees

Coaching is about being a Theory Y manager, and about assuming that each of your employees is able and willing to take responsibility for his or her performance or accept the consequences.

Alyce Johnson, in the Human Resources Department at MIT, tells us in an article entitled "What Is Coaching?" (web.mit.edu/hr/oed/learn/leading/art_coaching.html) that the practice is based on several basic assumptions:

- Employees want to succeed.
- Employees have ideas and want to share them with others on how work can be performed.
- Employees will expend effort to meet the goals they have a hand in formulating.
- Employees want to learn when they can see the value in terms of improved performance and success, along with accompanying recognition and rewards.

Do you remember the six beliefs or assumptions that I quoted in Chapter 1, taken from *Performance Management* by Robert Bacal? The following two seem worth repeating here in the context of coaching:

- Most employees, once they understand what's expected of them, will make every effort to meet those requirements.
- For the most part, if the manager does his or her job in supporting employees, each employee is really the resident expert about the job he or she does and how to improve performance.

What Is Coaching?

And how does Bacal define "coaching"? As "a process in which a person who is more knowledgeable on a particular issue works with an employee to help him or her develop knowledge and skills in order to improve performance" (*Performance Manage-ment*).

I like this definition, but I would quibble about "more knowledgeable on a particular issue" because a manager who is coaching may not be as knowledgeable about the details of a particular task his or her employee is doing, but knows more about the context within which the employee is doing that task ... and has the knowledge and authority (not to mention the responsibility) to help the employee.

Bacal also says, "When a manager plays the role of mentor, teacher, or helper, we usually call that 'coaching.'"

It's basically a matter of paying attention to each of your employees, looking for opportunities to praise and encourage or to help them improve. It's also, perhaps more important, about how you relate with your employees, how you communicate with each of them, how you help each of them communicate with you and with each other.

Coaching also maximizes the *Pygmalion effect*. You may be familiar with this term, which is one used for the phenomenon of people performing either up or down to what they believe that someone else expects of them. In other words, if your employees feel that you believe in them, they're likely to do better. If they feel you don't believe in them, you should expect them not to try so hard.

The **Pygmalion effect** is the way someone reacts to the expectations he or she knows or feels that another person has of him or her.

Management and organization development consultant Susan M. Heathfield has labeled the Pygmalion effect one of "the two most important management secrets." And what's the other important secret?

It's the *Galatea effect*—the result of self-expectations. What a person believes about his or her abilities does a lot to determine how well or poorly that person does. So, anything you can do to

---

The **Galatea effect** is the result of self-expectations. What a person believes about his or her abilities does a lot to determine how well or poorly that person does.

increase your employees' positive feelings about what they can achieve helps them achieve.

Heathfield includes the following suggestions among the ways that you can promote "positive, powerful self-expectations" in your employees ("The Two Most Important Management Secrets: The Pygmalion and Galatea Effects"):

- Provide one-to-one coaching. ... This coaching should emphasize improving what the employee does well rather than focusing on the employee's weaknesses.
- Hold frequent, positive verbal interactions with the employee and communicate consistently your firm belief in the employee's ability to perform the job.
- Keep feedback positive and developmental, where possible.
- Project your sincere commitment to the employee's success and ongoing development.

What Makes Coaching Effective?

Effective coaching is more about *how* you do things than *what* you do. So, before we discuss the things you should do, we need to consider the *attitude* and *approach* that make those *actions* more effective. These are some of the more important characteristics of a good coach:

- **Positive:** Focus on helping your employees develop their potential, not on correcting mistakes and finding fault.
- **Supportive:** Provide your employees what they need to do their jobs well (e.g., material resources, instructions, information, answers to questions, time, help overcoming obstacles, protection from interference).
- **Observant:** Be aware of what is happening and what isn't happening. Be attentive to what your employees are saying and what they aren't saying.
- **Enthusiastic:** Show interest in the work and positive energy.
- **Sensitive:** Care about how your employees feel, not just about how they do their work.
- **Honest:** Be frank about how your employees are doing. Admit

when you don't know something. Be honest with your employees as you expect them to be honest with you.

- **Respectful:** Treat your employees as humans, not just human resources.
- **Patient:** Allow your employees time to do what they need to do and time to say what they want to say.
- **Responsible:** Make sure your employees understand, whether that means understanding instructions, expectations, explanations, or whatever.

People talk about managing with carrots and sticks to get employees to perform. Sure, it's only a metaphor; managers would never think of their employees as beasts of burden. However, we can learn from people who actually work with beasts of burden. Anybody who knows horses and how to treat them well and get them to perform will tell you that success depends to a large extent on using words to connect with them and actions to guide them—and sensitivity to know what they need. That's how a manager should coach—not with carrots and sticks to motivate, but with words and actions and sensitivity.

Personal Issues

Sensitivity, however, should be balanced by sense. We should know that caring about our employees should not lead us into the dangerous area of their personal issues. As I mentioned in Chapter 7, it can be difficult to separate work performance problems from personal problems, but you must avoid any personal issues and focus only on performance issues.

It can be very difficult when you're coaching, since that means helping your employees overcome obstacles. On occasion, those obstacles may be personal issues and it may be your natural reaction to try to help with those obstacles as well.

Don't do it. This is a form of enabling. If you try to help, you make it less likely that your employee will take action to deal with those issues appropriately. That's his or her responsibility.

Delivering Doses of Coaching

A big question about coaching is whether to deliver the doses in meetings or on the spot, now and then, as the occasion arises.

If you coach in sessions, you can be more organized, it may be more efficient, you and your employee can be free from distractions, and you can talk one-to-one more easily away from other employees and distractions.

If you coach on the spot, you can deal with situations as they occur (the "rule" for feedback in general is that it be timely and specific) at the job site, so the employee can show you how he or she is doing a task or you can show how it could or should be done.

I think it's beneficial and often necessary to coach both ways, depending on the situation and the employee's needs. We'll first discuss the elements of coaching and then we'll outline the basics for conducting a coaching session.

Observing Your Employees

At the start of this chapter, I mentioned that the process of diagnosis and improvement should be continuous and one of the ways in which managers should be identifying problems is through simply paying attention, observing what's happening throughout their work unit.

You should not only try to find problems. In fact, if that's your purpose, employees will probably sense that and will assume you're trying to catch them doing something wrong—a common negative consequence of "managing by walking around" if it's done wrong.

You should simply check your territory, open to all that's happening. If you show the right attitude and you try, as Kenneth Blanchard famously put it, to catch your employees doing something right, then your employees should not feel anxious and, in fact, might feel comfortable taking the initiative to tell you about problems.

There are two additional advantages to managing by walking around: your employees have more opportunities to talk to you informally and they can more easily see you working (and being a good role model) than if you're isolated from them all of the time.

You may want to develop a form for jotting down things that you notice, to be sure that you capture all the pertinent facts about each situation (and to make sure that you note positive aspects as well as negative). There are forms in books and online that can guide you or that you can use as they are. However, no form is going to be appropriate for documenting everything you observe—and it may be human nature to tend to pay more attention to noticing and documenting situations that fit whatever form we're using. Also, it would be inconvenient to carry around a stack of forms whenever you walk around your work unit. It may be more practical to carry around a pad of paper and a pen, which you probably do already, and leave your forms in the office for use in writing up the situation and any ensuing discussion for your files.

You don't need to document all your coaching observations and discussions, of course. Sometimes you might notice something and then speak with the employee immediately for a moment. There's no need to document that intervention, unless it was particularly significant relative to one of his or her performance objectives or a continuing problem. If you're coaching in sessions rather than on the spot, you need to document more and probably in greater detail. Just try to be consistent in terms of what you decide to document.

Communicating with Your Employees

We discuss communication next, because however you coach, you will be using words. Even the late Marcel Marceau, a most talented mime, could not have coached effectively without words.

Here are some general recommendations on language to avoid and language to use. These are not rules or even advice for all occasions. I offer them simply as possibilities for communicating better with your employees.

Recommendation	Don't Say	Say
Focus on the solution, not the problem.	You did that wrong.	You can correct what happened by doing this.
Focus on the future, not the past.	I've told you several times not to ...	From now on ...
Be positive rather than negative.	I can't ...	What I can do is ...
	What I can't do is ...	I can promise you ...
	You can't do that now.	You can do that after you ...
	No, because ...	Yes, if ... or Yes, as soon as ...
	We can't do that.	We might be able to do that, provided ...
Say what you want, not what you don't want.	Don't hurry through the data entry and make mistakes.	Take the time you need to enter these figures correctly.
Make your point without sounding pushy.	You'll have to ... or You've got to ...	Could you ... or Would you be able to ... or replace "you" with "I"– What I need is for you to ... or replace "you" with "we"–We will have to ...
Be kind when you correct.	No, you're wrong.	I can understand why you did it like that ...
	That's not how to do it.	It works better if you do it this way.
Offer improvement suggestions rather than commenting on deficiencies.	You did this OK, except ...	If you do X, it would make it perfect.

Recommendation	Don't Say	Say
Avoid absolutes and generalizations.	You always get it wrong.	You've done this incorrectly several times, as I remember ...
	You never listen to me.	I don't know why I'm not explaining this well enough.
Avoid using the word "but" to connect statements if you can use the word "and."	I understand your point, but ...	I understand your point, and ...

It may seem like a lot to remember. However, I expect that you're already following some of these recommendations—at least when speaking with other managers, especially your superiors.

Importance of Being Open to Communication

Some managers talk a good game about promoting open, two-way communication with their employees—and yet it seems their office doors are generally closed. Others might as well be holed up in their offices when they're walking about looking so intensely lost in thought or obviously worrying that employees may not dare to approach them.

Sure, you're serious about your work and you always have serious work to do. If you need to close your door for quiet time but the work you're doing is not urgent life-or-death stuff, consider posting a sign that says, "Please Feel Free to Knock." And if you need to be out and about carrying the weight of your work unit on your head, remember to greet your employees as you pass. You'll still be able to be serious and do your work, but you'll probably seem more open to your employees—and more credible when you talk about open, two-way communication.

Perceiving and Processing and Thinking and Behaving

Communicating effectively requires realizing that each of us perceives things, processes those perceptions, thinks, and behaves in a unique way. We should be sensitive and alert to any indications that could tell us something about how the other person could better understand what we're trying to communicate.

There are many models based on theories and research. Here we will consider two of the most commonly used. This is a quick tour, emphasizing what you need to know and remember when communicating with your employees.

Learning Styles/Perceptual Modalities: VAK Model

A *perceptual modality* is the way in which the mind gets input. This is often called a *learning style*. We learn through all of our senses, but in each of us one sense tends naturally to dominate.

- **Visual** learners tend to learn best by seeing things. They learn better through images and pictures and drawings than from wordy explanations or discussions—unless those words are in writing. Visual learners create mental images.
- **Auditory** learners learn best through spoken words. They learn better when they hear information. Some need to repeat what they hear. Auditory learners carry mental images of spoken words and conversations.
- **Kinesthetic** learners and **tactile** learners. Kinesthetic learners learn best through sensing movement and position. Tactile learners learn best by touching.

There are ways to test for learning style. However, you can often get a sense of a person's learning style through oberservation. The smart manager always tries to find more than one way to communicate information. For example, give instructions orally, and then provide a printed version, and then, if possible, allow employees to actually do the task.

Experiential Learning Styles: Kolb Model

The Kolb model is a little more complicated, but worth understanding. There are two *preference dimensions—perception* and *processing*. Each dimension forms a continuum.

The **perception** dimension is about how people perceive reality around them. The continuum runs between concrete experience—perceiving things as they are, "in raw detail"—and abstract conceptualization—perceiving things as concepts and ideas, not the "raw detail" but an internal model.

The *processing* dimension is about how people take the results of their perception and process it. The continuum runs between *active experimentation*—taking what they have concluded and trying it out to prove that it works—and *reflective observation*—taking what they have concluded and watching to see if it works.

Now, we make one continuum vertical and the other continuum horizontal, forming a quadrant of four learning styles. (These styles derive from natural preferences and are not black and white labels, but tendencies in shades of gray.) In practical terms, that means communicating more effectively involves recognizing a person's experiential learning style and using the most appropriate means.

concrete experience + active experimentation = Accommodators

Accommodators have a strong preference for doing rather than thinking. They like to ask, "What if ...?" and "Why not ...?" They dislike routine. They tend to take creative risks to see what happens. Accommodators learn better when provided with hands-on experiences. They like practical learning rather than lectures.

concrete experience + reflective observation = Divergers

Divergers think deeply about experiences. They like to ask "Why?" and will start from details to work up to the big picture. Divergers learn better when allowed to observe and collect a range of information. They like to learn via logical instruction or hands-on exploration with conversations that lead to discovery.

abstract conceptualization + active experimentation = Convergers

Convergers think about things and then try out their ideas to see if they work. They like to ask "How ...?" and to understand how things work in practice. They like facts and they will try to make things more efficient by making small and careful changes. Convergers learn better when provided with practical applications of concepts and theories. They prefer to work by themselves, thinking carefully and acting independently.

abstract conceptualization + reflective observation =
Assimilators

Assimilators have the most cognitive approach, preferring to think than to act. They like organized and structured understanding. They ask, "What is there I can know?" They prefer lectures for learning, with demonstrations if possible, and generally respect the knowledge of experts. Assimilators learn better when they can start with high-level concepts and work down to the details.

If you are interested in knowing more about how our minds work differently and how we can use what we know to communicate more effectively, I recommend getting information on the Myers-Briggs Type Indicator (personality types) and the DISC model (personality styles).

Motivating Your Employees

We begin our discussion of coaching with motivating. Why? According to Theory Y, you should assume that most or all of your employees are motivated to work and even to do their best to meet expectations. You want to support and build that motivation from the start.

"Motivating employees starts with motivating yourself." That's the first principle, according to Carter McNamara, a partner in Authenticity Consulting, LLC ("Basics About Employee Motivation"). "Enthusiasm is contagious. If you're enthusiastic about your job, it's much easier for others to be, too."

In General

In Chapter 7, I presented the Motivation-Hygiene Hypothesis formulated by Frederick Herzberg. The essential takeaway from that hypothesis is that managers should do two things:

1. Try to decrease the negative effects of dissatisfiers (factors that affect motivation negatively more by their absence than positively by their presence). Basically, be alert to any concerns or complaints or even questions employees might have about working conditions, interpersonal relations, safety and security, the policies and administration of the organization, and—last but probably most important—how you manage.

2. Try action to increase the positive effects of satisfiers (factors that drive motivation—"the more, the better"). This means helping them achieve, recognizing them for their achievements, boosting their interest in the job, allowing for greater responsibility, and providing for advancement and growth.

How do your employees feel about things that Herzberg labeled "dissatisfiers"? If you don't know, ask them. If you think you know, check with them. The same is true for the factors labeled as "satisfiers." That, however, generally seems to be an individual matter.

As Individuals

I mentioned in the discussion of rewards and recognition in Chapter 7 that Anne Bruce includes in her book *Building a High-Morale Workplace* a survey to assess factors that may affect employee morale. I suggested it might be a good idea to develop a similar survey for your employees. At this point, in the context of motivation, I return to that idea—with two twists.

You could take a few minutes to list all the things you think could be motivating your employees. Then add a few blank lines, for additions to the list. This is now a survey. Here's the first twist: instead of asking your employees to *rate* the items listed, ask them to *rank* the top five. Now, here's the second twist: ask them to put their names on the survey forms.

If they are honest, you will know for each employee what makes him or her tick at work. You will know which satisfiers you need to be increasing to motivate that employee.

Guiding Your Employees

Coaching always involves guiding to some extent. That means guiding each of your employees in terms of the following:

- Specific tasks and responsibilities
- Objectives of his or her performance plan
- His or her performance improvement plan (if any)

Should you also guide each employee in terms of his or her personal development plan?

Personal development is ... well, personal. Each of your employees has different interests and is motivated in different ways to pursue those interests. What you do to help an employee depends on how that employee wants to develop and how he or she wants you to help and, of course, what help he or she is willing to accept from you at any particular moment. So what you would do in coaching is not so much guiding but following and providing support.

> **Coaching Is a Separate Activity**
> Just as it makes sense to discuss personal development separately from job performance in meetings following performance appraisals and to create personal development objectives separately from performance objectives, it may generally make sense to try to maintain that separation while coaching.
>
> So you might not want to ask, in the middle of discussing a performance issue, "So, how's it going with your interest in studying taxidermy online?" However, you should be aware of situations in which it would be appropriate to mention some aspect of an employee's personal development plan in the context of discussing a closely related job task.

Depending on the situation and the individual, guiding could involve training, offering suggestions, making recommendations, providing resources (including information and time), removing obstacles, and shielding from interference.

Asking the Right Questions and Asking Questions Right

I've put this section on asking questions before the section on using feedback. That's because you should usually begin a coaching conversation with questions, so you understand the situation from your employee's perspective. Remember Habit 5 from *The 7 Habits of Highly Effective People* by Stephen R. Covey: "Seek first to understand, then to be understood."

It's important to be able to approach your employees and start asking questions casually. You can start with a very general question, like "How are things going?" You may have to ask it more than once and maybe vary the wording so the employees don't take it as just a greeting. If the answer is "OK" or "Fine," you should ask more specific questions. It may not be easy, but when your employees realize that you really are interested in their work and in helping them do it more easily, to actually facilitate it, they should start answering your questions.

Casual Questions

In *Perfect Phrases for Managers and Supervisors* (McGraw-Hill, 2005), Meryl Runion suggests trying casual questions like the following:

- How's it going?
- What's on your mind?
- Hey, I like the way you ____!
- It's always great to see you.
- By the way, great job on ____.
- Is there anything you need from me?
- How comfortable is your workload?
- Is there anything you want me to know?

When you ask questions within a coaching context, keep in mind that an effective question is:

- **Brief.** The longer the question, the easier it is to go wrong. The most obvious problem would be confusing the employee.
- **Focused.** Target one specific thing. Avoid going astray and stringing together a series of questions, e.g., "Do you think you should do X or should you maybe try Y or I guess Z is also possible, right?" How would the employee answer that multiple question? How would he or she even remember all of it?
- **Relevant.** Stay on task. It's more efficient and less likely to

encourage your employee to digress. (If an answer strays off the point, paraphrase the words that come closest to answering your question.) Generally, a question should not come out of nowhere, unless you're trying to surprise or shake up the employee (if, for example, he or she seems to be sticking to a "script").

- **Clear.** Use simple language and simple sentence structure. Your goal is to communicate, not impress or confuse or frustrate.

- **Positive.** This simply means getting the higher return on investment and causing the least collateral emotional damage. In other words, try using the advice offered earlier on the language to use and the language to avoid.

When your question elicits an answer, you may want or need to find out more. You should develop the art of asking probing questions, whether to get details, evidence, or opinions or whatever else.

Here are some examples of probing questions:

- Could you be more specific?
- What happened then?
- What do you think might have caused that to happen?
- Can you give me an example of that?
- For instance?
- And you think that's not a good idea because ...?
- Could you explain what you mean by that?
- How does this affect you?
- Can you fill me in on the details?

These questions are all brief, focused, relevant, clear, and positive. Good! However, when you ask probing questions, it's not about being effective. When you probe, your tone of voice and speaking rhythm should remain normal. You don't want your employee to feel like you don't trust his or her answers or you're not paying attention or you're conducting a police interrogation.

I should add that probing with "why" questions can be especially difficult. This is generally because "Why?" can be asking for either an *explanation* or a *justification.* Usually people are comfortable if you ask for an explanation but usually not if you want a justification. And sometimes people will assume the worst, that you're challenging them. If you ask a question like "Why do you think that?" or "Why did you do that?" you've got to be very careful with your tone of voice, your expression, and your body language.

Asking good questions is one of the best tools for coaching effectively. But be careful. "Avoid asking questions in staccato bursts," Marshall J. Cook and Laura Poole advise in their book, *Effective Coaching* (2nd Ed.) "and avoid rhetorical questions, fill-in-the-blank questions, and pointed questions."

Rhetorical questions are asked not to elicit an answer but rather to manipulate the other person. As Cook and Poole note, "They may get you hostility instead of dialog and cooperation."

What these authors call "fill-in-the-blank" questions are those that are asked to get answers that the person asking the question already knows. The effect is invariably to make the other person feel like a child. "How do you answer the phone?" "XYX Inc." "That's right. And then what do you say?" "How may I help you?" "Good! And then how do you end the call?" If you know the answer, don't ask the question. If you want to know if the employee knows the answer, ask "Do you know how to ...?"

Finally, *pointed* questions are simply statements that end with a question tag, such as "right" or words to that effect. For example, "You wouldn't really do that, would you?" or "You know better, don't you?"

Cook and Poole end their comments on the three questions to avoid with simple advice: "Ask *real* questions that need *real* answers, and you'll do fine." To which I add, "And be careful with your tone of voice and speaking rhythm."

Listening

We discussed listening actively in Chapter 5, so we don't need to discuss it much here.

Instead, I invite you to assess your listening behaviors. For each item check the box that's most appropriate.

While Someone Is Talking ...	Usually	Sometimes	Rarely
1. I nod or say things like "Uh-huh" to get the person to continue.			
2. I plan what I'm going to say next.			
3. I maintain eye contact with the person.			
4. I try to sense the feelings behind the words.			
5. I think about other things on my schedule.			
6. I pay attention to body language (expressions and gestures).			
7. I interrupt if I need to make a point.			
8. I take notes, as appropriate.			
9. I help finish sentences if the person pauses.			
10. I try not to immediately evaluate what the person is saying.			
11. I interrupt to ask questions when I need more information.			
12. I wait for the person to pause and then I paraphrase what he or she has just said, to make sure I understand.			

For behaviors 1, 3, 4, 6, 8, 10, and 12: the **more** often, the better.
For behaviors 2, 5, 7, 9, and 11: the **less** often, the better.

Sometimes people are listening well and actively, but their body language sends signals that suggest otherwise. So, how can your body language show that you're listening? Here are some things to keep in mind.

- Lean toward the speaker slightly. Research has shown that when people are sitting face to face talking, leaning backward suggests a feeling of dominance while leaning forward shows interest.
- Don't check your watch. This makes it seem like you're impatient. If you do it while the other person is talking, it can sug-

gest that you're not so interested in what he or she is saying.

- Keep looking up at the other person if you're taking notes while he or she is speaking. Write quickly and keep pausing, so your note-taking doesn't become a distraction for either of you.
- Vary the ways in which you express interest nonverbally, whether by nodding or saying "Uh-huh" or whatever. You don't want your signs of interest to seem mechanical, like you're on auto pilot.
- Be careful not to react emotionally to what the person is saying, as your emotion may show on your face.

Using Feedback with Your Employees

The mention of this one word, "feedback," usually triggers the mention of two more words, "positive" and "negative" (or "constructive" and "critical").

Does that conventional distinction hold? Is this area black and white or is feedback a continuum?

How would you label the following examples of feedback as positive or negative?

- Well, you're doing a good job—finally!
- You're still doing it wrong, but I've got confidence you can do it right.
- Your performance here seems just about adequate.

Our focus is to avoid the positive-negative distinction. What matters is this:

- Be honest.
- Express with respect whatever you choose to say.
- Be sensitive to the person's feelings.

Providing Feedback

The first rule of providing feedback in coaching should be "Know what's happening." Even if you think you know all the facts of a situation, get your employee's perspective.

Then you can decide whether to provide feedback immediately or to hold it for a coaching session. If you decide to talk with your employee later, take notes on the task or behavior and the specific circumstances. If you decide to talk with your employee immediately, do it privately, away from your other employees. I recommend doing so whether your feedback is positive or negative. I won't question the general wisdom of the advice given by football coach and philosopher Vince Lombardi, "Praise in public, criticize in private." However, if you're giving substantive feedback, privacy seems better, if only so your employee can focus better on your words.

To provide feedback effectively, you should consider the following questions:

- How is your employee expected to perform?
- Does your employee understand these expectations? If not, why not?
- Does your employee recognize the results of performing according to expectations?
- Does your employee know that his or her performance is unsatisfactory?
- Are there factors interfering with performing? Can you reduce the effects of those factors or remove them?
- Has your employee ever performed this task satisfactorily?
- Does performing satisfactorily mean that the workload is increased?
- Does performing unsatisfactorily mean positive consequences, such as assignment of an easier task or reassignment of an undesirable task to another employee?

In *Building a High-Morale Workplace,* Anne Bruce says that when managers make a point of giving employees regular feedback, it sends "a much bigger message.... 'I care about you and want to help you develop your talents.'"

Bruce recommends that managers who want to help their employees develop should know how to provide four types of feedback:

1. Frequent and sincere
2. Fast and action-oriented (aka "speedback")
3. Helpful and corrective: "The point here is to be constructive and not destructive"
4. Empathetic and sincere

In giving feedback, be specific. Also, whenever possible, recognize the efforts of your employee. And remember: "Help people reach their full potential: catch them doing something right" (Ken Blanchard, *The One-Minute Manager*) and then praise them immediately.

This section on providing feedback continues in a later section, "Coaching in Sessions."

The title of this section is "Using Feedback with Your Employees." I chose that wording because "using" applies not only to feedback you provide to your employees but also to feedback you get from them.

Getting Feedback

There are two dimensions to getting feedback:

- How you encourage your employees to give you feedback
- How you handle the "gift"

Yes, you should accept feedback as a gift. That may not come easily, but when you request and welcome feedback and accept it with appreciation, you can serve as a model for your employees.

Here's some advice from Linda Dulye, President and Founder of Dulye & Co. ("View Feedback as a Gift," *dulye.com*): By changing your view of feedback, you'll also enhance how much value you get from it.

Her recommendations include:

- **Be gracious.** Accept the feedback as you would a gift; even if that means setting it aside for a while before realizing its value.
- **Be open-minded.**
- **Say thank you.** Not everyone feels comfortable giving feedback. While it's always important to thank those who express

their ideas on a subject, it's also especially important to acknowledge those who do so when they are out of their comfort zone.

Try focusing on that last point. You have much more experience thanking people than accepting feedback, so let that feeling of familiarity provide some reassurance. If you pay attention to the feedback and then thank the "gift-giver" immediately, you can shift your mind away from the gift until you can consider it in private, even, as Dulye notes, if you need to wait a while before you realize the value of that gift.

"It's always smart to acknowledge and consider the feedback you get from employees," Anne Bruce says, "whether you choose to act on it or not. ... Every time an employee offers you feedback, you have another opportunity to improve the environment and improve yourself" (*Building a High-Morale Workplace*).

When an employee gives you feedback:

- Try to remain calm, open, and positive.
- Thank your employee for showing an interest.
- Paraphrase to show that you understand.
- Ask your employee what you can do to improve the situation.
- Paraphrase to show that you understand (e.g., "So, you're suggesting that if I do ABC, then XYZ will happen?")
- Thank your employee again.

When he was mayor of New York City, Ed Koch was famous for always asking everyone he met, "How'm I doing?" He must have been doing well enough, since he was elected for three terms. You probably don't want to do that around your work unit. But there are other ways.

First, if you're coaching employees on their job performance, "The best way to judge how effectively you're communicating with employees," according to Cook and Poole "is ... to observe their subsequent performance." You may also be able to get a sense by the way they react with you after you give them feedback.

If you get into the good habit of asking your employees questions casually, as recommended earlier, they are likely to feel more comfortable answering honestly, so you can include casual questions to get feedback about how you're doing. Here's a "perfect phrase" from Runion (*Perfect Phrases for Managers and Supervisors*): "When I improve as a manager, your job gets easier. That's why I need your feedback."

Of course, if you show that you're accepting feedback as a gift, your employees will be more comfortable giving it. If an employee makes a suggestion you decide to adopt that will improve the workplace, you could make a point of mentioning it at the next meeting and thanking the employee again. Something like that can truly motivate your employees to give you feedback.

Action Steps for Coaching Something New

Sometimes you will need to teach an employee how to do something. It may be a new task, procedure, or skill, or it may be something the employee has had so much trouble doing that it seems best to start from zero.

Here are five steps to guide you in coaching your employee to do X, whatever it may be.

1. Prepare the employee.
   - Introduce—with sensitivity—the need for you to coach him or her on doing X.
   - Seek the employee's commitment to improving by learning to do X.
   - Ask for ideas and suggestions.
   - Review details of previous performance.
   - Establish with the employee goals for the learning session.

2. Demonstrate or describe the desired performance.
   - Work from the simple to the complex.
   - Review the desired performance, using examples.
   - Explain the key steps in achieving the goal.
   - Role-play correct behaviors.
   - Give a hands-on demonstration.
   - Have the employee talk your instructions back to you.

3. Create a positive atmosphere.
   - Reassure the employee about his or her potential for doing X.
   - Share problems you experienced in learning to do X.
   - Encourage the employee to express concerns and listen to them.
   - Provide a safety net for taking risks.
   - Communicate your high expectations to the employee.

4. Have the employee do X.
   - Ensure a low-risk setting for practice.
   - Videotape the performance for detailed coaching later.
   - Provide all the resources and supplies necessary.
   - Keep a low profile while the employee is trying to do X.
   - Avoid body language or words that could interfere with practice.
   - Check whether the employee has any concerns or questions.

5. Follow up.
   - Praise and congratulate the employee.
   - Provide timely, detailed feedback.
   - Make sure the employee plans to continue practicing.
   - Schedule additional coaching as needed.
   - Ask the employee for suggestions to improve your coaching skills.

A checklist may help your employee remember procedures and specifics. You could even start with a copy of the instructions and highlight the most important words or sentences. You could monitor your employee's progress and then, as he or she improves, replace the highlighted instructions with a checklist.

Monitoring Your Employees' Progress

Monitor and document the progress of each of your employees in terms of his or her performance plan and performance improvement plan. Also remind your employees to make notes and keep records of their progress and achievement. This makes it easier to prepare for the performance appraisal.

Consider creating a status board to track each employee's progress toward his or her performance objectives. Design a board you can update easily that will serve as a quick visual reminder to check on your employees regularly.

Coaching in Sessions

To prepare for a coaching session, write up a list of issues or performance areas you want to discuss. This will serve as the meeting agenda. It's better to list only a few, so you can discuss them adequately. If your employee has improved significantly in any area, include that on your list. Organize the items in a way that seems appropriate, such as in terms of your employee's performance objectives, past performance problems, or in order of importance. You should also have your documentation, notes on your employee's performance, with examples. Finally, write out an overall assessment of your employee, like a quick "balance sheet" of his or her current situation. Keep it general and short, an "executive summary" of 25 words or less.

Make sure there will be no interruptions or other distractions. Turn off your monitor and your telephone and put away any devices, such as your cell phone.

Welcome your employee, but keep the social amenities to a minimum. Delay will probably make your employee feel uncomfortable. Commend your employee on any significant achievement or improvement. It's good to start the session on a positive note. Just don't overdo it.

Transition into your agenda with the overall assessment you've prepared. This enables your employee to know in a few words what you think of his or her current job performance.

Then, follow your agenda. Make a point, calmly (e.g., "I've noticed that ... ") and briefly. Pause for a moment to let it register. Then cite your evidence and examples. Be specific about the situations where you observed the performance issue in question. Pause after each one, long enough so your employee can remember the instance. You may be able to judge by how he or she reacts, but you may need to ask, "Do you remember doing that?" The more specifically you describe the situation, the better your employee may remember the circumstances and maybe the factors that caused the problem.

Next, ask for a reaction, e.g., "What do you think about that?" or "Would you agree with that point?" Avoid asking your employee to explain, to justify, or to respond in any specific way. Leave it open so your employee feels free to react.

Take notes on reactions as well as on the ensuing discussion. This should be like taking minutes during a business meeting.

Discuss the points your employee raises. However, avoid disagreement or confrontation. Keep in mind that your goal is to help your employee perform better, not to win arguments. If you feel that a point isn't worth discussing, for whatever reason, at least acknowledge it (e.g., "I understand that you are annoyed by that procedure ...") and move on ("I realize that you don't understand the instructions. So, let's talk about that."). Coaching sessions should be two-way communication, open and honest. Just avoid dead ends and bogs. Also, direct the discussion toward the future, away from the past.

If you want to disagree with something your employee has said or to move on to something different, first paraphrase what he or she has said, to make sure you've understood it correctly, and then say what you want to say.

You may want to ask specific questions about causes identified during the performance diagnosis meeting. Remain relaxed and friendly, even if you feel that your employee should be making more progress. Ask about obstacles and whether he or she needs other resources.

If your employee expresses concern or frustration over factors that he or she feels are impeding improvement, listen and respond with empathy. Ask probing questions to investigate those factors and try to come up with ways to deal with them. It's best to work together, but your employee may feel unable to do anything, so it may be up to you.

For each performance problem you discuss, agree on actions either of you will be taking. Allow your employee to lead the way here, if possible. Ask leading questions, such as "So, now what can you do in order to do X better?" and "And what can I do to help you do X better?" Make note of any action plans you make together.

After you finish discussing the final point on your agenda, you should ask your employee to sign it to acknowledge that the two of you have discussed the items listed. Schedule a follow-up meeting or next coaching session.

Thank your employee (e.g., "Thank you for talking with me about how things have been going lately ... "). Then add a specific comment to end on a personal note:

- "I appreciate your efforts with X, and I hope our talk will help you do X even better."
- "I know you've had difficulties doing Y, but you're making good progress now."
- "I feel like you're going to be able to achieve your objective for Z. Keep up the good work!"

Follow up on the coaching session by giving your employee a copy of the agenda and, if you choose, a copy of your notes ("minutes").

You may decide that it would be more effective and/or fit your schedule better to focus on a single issue or performance area in your coaching sessions. Focusing may be necessary, particularly for an employee who seems overwhelmed and unable to deal with various factors affecting his or her performance. If the session is to discuss just one issue or area, you should be able to come up with action plans so specific that your employee will leave the session inspired and completely focused on taking action.

Documenting Coaching Sessions

If you decide to do coaching sessions focused on a single issue or area, it may be easier for you to document your coaching. There are forms that you can download and use, although I would recommend adapting them to your circumstances and needs, if not in advance then at least after you've tried them out.

A basic form might look like the following:

Coaching Session Form		
Name:	**Date:**	**Start Time:** **End Time:**
Where Coaching Needed:		
Problem (Skill Deficiency, Performance Problem):		
Desired Outcomes:		
Importance of the Issue (Effects, Potential Consequences)		
Problems and How to Address Them:		
Actions to Take (Who will do what by when):		
Manager: _____ **Employee:** _____		

You can also evaluate the coaching session for your records. A basic form might include material as shown on the form on the next page.

It's smart to document coaching sessions as you would any other meeting, especially when there are action plans or other commitments. Your documentation (signed by your employee) constitutes a record of your efforts to help your employee

Coaching Results		
Name:	Date:	Start Time: End Time:
Notes on Relationship with Employee **What felt right?** **What felt wrong?**		
Notes on Coaching Session **What worked well?** **What needs improvement?**		

improve—a record that could provide some protection if the situation with an employee gets worse and leads to discipline or, ultimately, termination.

Do It Right
Before you document your coaching sessions, you should check with your human resources department, which may have specific procedures and required forms.

If you document coaching sessions, document sessions with all of your employees. Even if you suspect that one of your employees will continue to perform poorly and is likely to be leaving the organization in the near future, if you document coaching sessions with only that one employee and not the others, that special consideration could be used against you in a claim of discriminatory treatment.

Positive Coaching Sessions
You may have occasion to conduct a coaching session to provide positive feedback. Your procedure should be much the same as for any other coaching session, with some differences.

Describe the positive performance. Be specific. Then ask questions to determine how your employee has improved, his or her "success story." Depending on the job tasks and the causes you and the employee had identified for the performance problem, you may want to ask about certain aspects in particular or ask more general questions. You want to know what worked: training, understanding expectations better, more resources, support from coworkers, greater effort, more time, excellent coaching.

Discuss how your employee can continue doing well and whether you can help. Express your appreciation for the positive performance and mention the effects on your work unit and the organization.

Document the coaching session, as usual, but think about whether any of the factors that helped this one employee succeed could help other employees.

Applying a Little Pressure

It may be necessary at some time, more likely at a follow-up discussion of a continuing performance issue, to apply a little pressure. You may suspect that it will not be enough to show your concern and offer help. You may realize that the problem is not so much an issue of abilities or aptitude, but something else, something the employee should be able to overcome.

Ask your employee to explain why he or she hasn't made sufficient progress. (The explanation may indicate that the employee is unlikely to try to do better.) Then, mention a negative consequence of continuing to perform unsatisfactorily.

Any negative consequences you mention should be possible and natural results of the problem in question, rather than any actions you could impose on your employee. Be specific. Never state a negative consequence that won't happen. That will weaken your position.

What negative consequences could you mention? If performance is below expectations and you deem it necessary to push for improvement, it should generally be because the performance gap is causing something bad to happen. Why are you pushing your employee to improve? There also could be negative consequences that may not be natural results, but would be logical. For example:

- If you don't improve, it's going to be necessary for me to be spending more time helping you with your work. (In other words, I'll be a presence that makes you uncomfortable if you don't do your job better.)
- If you don't improve, I'll be forced to find another assignment that's more ... challenging/tedious. (In other words, you're going to be moved to a job you may like even less.)

Don't use a threatening tone. The purpose of stating negative consequences is to change the unsatisfactory behavior or performance; it's not to punish your employee. Don't make threats. This isn't to be an oral warning and the start of the progressive discipline process, although you should be treating the discussion as if it could be the last step before you start progressive discipline.

Again, you should agree on the actions the employee commits to taking and the time frame, which should be as short as feasible, and actions you will take, which might include spot checks. Schedule a meeting to follow up on the actions, making it as soon as appropriate. Tell your employee that you are confident that he or she can improve. Document your follow-up discussion, of course, including your employee's explanation of the performance problem and any negative consequences you mention.

Dealing with Employee Problems

"Discipline" is defined by Robert Bacal in *Performance Management* as "*the process used to address performance problems*; it involves the manager in identifying and communicating performance problems to employees, and in identifying, communicating, and applying consequences if the performance problems are not remedied." He adds that the discipline process, in its early stages, is like the performance management process. However, when a manager and an employee are not able to remedy a performance problem working together, then the manager must deal with the problem "with other tools, which may involve unilateral action, maybe the application of 'consequences.'"

We've already considered the use of negative consequences, which can be either natural results of the performance problem or actions that a manager will take because of it. If the employee doesn't improve under the pressure of negative consequences, then the manager may have no choice but to use a progressive discipline process.

As mentioned in Chapter 7, a progressive discipline process is a program for dealing with employee problems through activities intended to modify behavior by applying a series of increasingly severe punishments for unacceptable behavior. There are various sequences used and the terms may be defined in different ways.

oral warning	oral reprimand	informal verbal warning documented in a log
formal oral warning with documentation	written warning	formal verbal warning
written warning	final written warning	written warning
final warning	termination review	written warning with disciplinary action (e.g., suspension or demotion)
termination	termination	termination

You should know the specific process established by your human resources office—and you should use it. A progressive discipline process is the best way to remedy persistent employee performance problems.

However, a process is only as good as the actions taken. If there are no negative consequences and if disciplinary actions are only warnings and reprimands and papers in a file, you may be encouraging poor performance. So, know the procedures for the progressive discipline process in your organization—and make it work.

Your organization's progressive discipline process is not only the most effective way to address persistent performance problems, it's also the best way to protect against legal actions for wrongful termination. If you follow the process and document all your actions properly, according to the requirements in the procedures, you ensure that any employee you terminate for not meeting specified performance expectations was treated fairly and in accordance with your organization's policies.

Appraise Your Performance as Coach

I recently found a self-evaluation checklist for coaches that consists of two dozen questions to be answered by Yes or No. My immediate reaction was "Would you use a simple checklist like this to evaluate your employees?"

First of all, it's Yes-No. That seems far too simplistic, particularly for a self-evaluation. That raises a second question: "Would you give your employees this form to rate you?" That consideration should make you wonder if there's a better rating scale for this evaluation than Yes-No. Sure, this evaluation form is quick: it might take only as long to answer the questions as it takes to read them. It seems like assessing your coaching performance is important enough to warrant an investment of more than a few minutes.

Another concern is that all 25 questions are to be answered with a Yes. Since it's human nature to want to feel good about yourself, this self-evaluation tool is virtually a invitation to managers to simply "check the boxes" and feel good about how well they're coaching their employees.

I dislike being negative, but it's essential to think carefully about the tools you use. There are so many resources available in books and magazines and on websites that we should be able to find the most appropriate for our purposes.

You could also develop your own self-assessment form. Choose the best items from whatever self-assessment forms you find and then add items you need to make it more complete and more suitable for your particular situation. Here are some examples:

- I try to develop a supportive, emotional relationship with my employees.
- I am attentive about observing what my employees are doing.
- I take advantage of coaching opportunities as I notice them.
- I listen actively to my employees.

- I avoid assuming anything or judging my employees until I get the facts.
- I use open questions to encourage my employees to communicate more.
- I check my understanding of what my employees say by repeating or paraphrasing.
- I try to help my employees find ways to improve their skills.
- The feedback I provide is timely.
- The feedback I provide is specific.
- I try to catch my employees doing something right.
- I try to balance my feedback with both positive and negative.
- After I coach an employee, I follow up to check on whether he or she is doing better.

Then set up a rating scale of between four and seven points. For example, here's a five-point scale with percentages quantifying adverbs—"On occasions when it would be appropriate, indicate when you do each of the following items:"

- always: 90 percent–100 percent
- usually: 65 percent–90 percent
- frequently: 35 percent–65 percent
- sometimes: 10 percent–35 percent
- never: 0 percent–10 percent

Would it be more difficult to use this rating scale than to check Yes or No? Absolutely. But it also seems more realistic. Also, assessing how you're coaching should require more thinking about the questions than if you're choosing between Yes and No.

You could then add a diagnostic, some follow-up questions: How well is it working? When you do this, how well does it work? When you don't, what are your reasons for not doing it?

Next, logically, you could put a question about improving: How could you do better on this item?

How long would it take you to complete this three-part self-assessment? If you take your coaching responsibilities seriously and you really want to improve, it seems worth investing the time and effort in evaluating your performance.

9 Managing Teams and Performance Appraisal

W hen you are working with teams, the performance appraisal process starts as soon as you begin to form the team and/or as soon as the team has a purpose and goals. The function of the "and/or" depends on whether you intend to evaluate the employees who are becoming members of the team, the team itself, or both. Here we discuss all three possibilities.

Working Definition

Team A team is a group of people working together toward specific objectives within a defined operational sphere (Lawrence Holpp, *Managing Teams* [McGraw-Hill, 1999]).

In the Beginning

Since this chapter focuses on performance appraisal with teams, we won't enter into general aspects of forming a team. (For that, I recommend *The Team Handbook* by Peter R. Scholtes, Brian L. Joiner, and Barbara J. Streibel.) Instead, we will focus on the purpose and goals of the team.

Performance Appraisal

When you evaluate the performance of the team, you use as the criteria the goals set for the team. That seems logical and—if the goals are specific and measurable—straightforward.

How do you appraise the performance of each of the members of the team? You set objectives in two categories—*shared* and *individual*—to guide performance and to serve as the basis for performance appraisal.

You should set one or more shared objectives for all of the members based on the team purpose and goals. These could be simply statements of equally shared responsibility, such as "Contributed at least 10 percent to the achievement of the team goal of X," if the team consisted of 10 members.

You may want to also set shared objectives based on the team behaviors you expect, especially if they are covered by ground rules set by or for the team. For example:

- The team members will cooperate with each other.
- The team members will attend all full team meetings.
- The team members will participate actively in all meetings.
- The team members will report to the manager significant problems that arise.

You should also set specific objectives for each member according to his or her role(s) and responsibilities. (This process is similar to the process for developing performance objectives for employees from work unit goals and organization goals.) If there are no established roles and responsibilities for team members, I'd suggest setting objectives based on the experience and skills that each member will contribute to the team effort.

For Example

In "Managing the Performance of Teams—Two Critical Dimensions," Bob Selden, author of *What to Do When You Become the Boss*, discusses setting performance standards or expectations for individual team members and for the team. He says that both individual and team performance standards should include:

- Descriptions of the "expected behaviors" ("often known as *process measures*")
- Descriptions of the "results required" ("known as *output measures*")

Process measures for each *team member* could include how well he or she does the following:

- cooperates with the other members
- shares experiences with the other members
- suggests solutions for team problems
- communicates his or her ideas during team meetings
- participates in making team decisions
- helps out other team members when they need it

Output measures for each *team member* could include such items as the following:

- quality of a team member's written report of team results
- turnaround time for a team member's contribution needed by the team
- accuracy of the advice the team member supplies to the team

Process measures for the *team* could include how well the members as a team:

- run meetings effectively
- communicate during meetings
- allow all members to voice their opinions
- reach consensus on decisions
- share leadership authority as needed

Output measures for the *team* could include such items as:

- satisfaction rate of customers or other stakeholders with the team's products or services
- percentage decline of team backlog items
- cycle time for the team's entire work processes

For team performance standards, Selden says it's "imperative" that the team members develop these together. He suggests "running a team session to set the performance expectations."

Assessing Team Development

Assessment of the team should generally start from the beginning of the team—from the inside.

You should be able to do this easily with a short survey. List a few basic questions, such as the examples below. Distribute copies of your survey to your team members at the end of the first team meeting. Ask them to answer the questions honestly—and anonymously, of course. Although the questions are Yes/No, you can invite them to add any explanations or any concerns.

Examples:

- Do you understand the team purpose and goals?
- Do you feel that the team members seem committed to the team, its purpose, and its goals?
- Do you feel that the team can fulfill its purpose and achieve its goals with the support and resources provided?

These three questions are generic, good for any team. You will want to include questions appropriate to your situation, the structure of the team, its purpose, its objectives, and so on.

Post It

Post the team purpose and goals around the work area. If the team members have established roles and responsibilities on the team, post those as well.

Use surveys like the initial one from time to time as the team develops and progresses. You may want to do this regularly, at the end of every meeting of the full team, depending on the frequency of the meetings. If there are meetings of subgroups, you could use surveys with those, too.

On those subsequent surveys add questions specific to the activities and development of the team, particularly if there are difficulties or issues. Here are some examples, beginning with a more general question:

- Have you noticed problems with any of the team members? If so, please name the members and describe the problem.

- Are any members failing to fulfill their responsibilities to the team?
- Is any member dominating the other members?
- Are any members trying to assume roles beyond the ones assigned to them?

How should you handle problems or issues that are reported? That may depend on how many reports you receive on any team member (either through the assessments or otherwise) and the effects, the timing (relative to team development and status of progress toward team goals), and the causes of the problems or issues.

It's probably not advisable to meet with the members in question, since that could make the situation worse, especially if the members in question assume they know who reported them. The best course might be to take a little time during a subsequent meeting to discuss, in general terms, issues that commonly arise in teams, such as misunderstandings about roles and responsibilities.

However, if you notice problems or issues (and you might decide to be more attentive if you receive any reports), then it's probably best to meet with the members in question, as you would do with employees in a conventional work situation. Again, consider such factors as the effects, the timing, and the causes of the problems or issues.

Exhibit 9-1 shows an example of an assessment form.

Assessing Team Behavior

It's a good idea to regularly assess your team in terms of expected behaviors, particularly if you've established any behaviors as ground rules, whether for team activities in general, for specific team functions, or for team meetings.

You can assess team behavior yourself or you can also have the team members provide their perspectives. Start with your list of behaviors; if you don't have one, it's time to make a list. (It's usually best to have between 5 and 10, enough to cover most general aspects of teamwork but not so many as to be hard to keep in

Team Effectiveness	Circle Rating					
1. Team goals seem unclear.	1	2	3	4	5	Team goals seem very clear.
2. Membership: "I feel excluded."	1	2	3	4	5	Membership: "I feel included."
3. Elbow room: "I feel crowded."	1	2	3	4	5	Elbow room: "I feel comfortable."
4. Discussions: "I'm cautious and guarded."	1	2	3	4	5	Discussions: "I'm open and free."
5. Use of skills poor.	1	2	3	4	5	Use of skills extensive.
6. Support for self only.	1	2	3	4	5	Support for all members.
7. Conflicts: "We avoid dealing with them."	1	2	3	4	5	Conflicts: "We work on them."
8. Only a few members influence opinions.	1	2	3	4	5	All members influence decisions.

Exhibit 9-1. An Example of a Team Assessment Form

mind.) Behaviors usually cover such aspects of group dynamics as respect and cooperation. Here's an example with a few standard items.

Team members are expected:

- To treat each other with respect and dignity
- To be punctual for meetings
- To participate actively in meetings
- To respect the right of other members to propose ideas and offer suggestions
- To complete action items as scheduled
- To ...

Once you've listed the expected behaviors, it's easy to turn them into an assessment form like the one at the top of the next page.

Pass out copies of your assessment at full team meetings or to team members individually (in person, by memo, by e-mail, etc.). Ask them to complete the assessment honestly and—again—anonymously.

Rate the team for each of the following behaviors, from 1 (low) to 5 (high).
Team members treat each other with respect and dignity.   _____
Team members are punctual for meetings.   _____
Team members participate actively in meetings.   _____
Team members respect the right of other members to propose
ideas and offer suggestions.   _____
Team members are completing action items as scheduled.   _____
Team members ...   _____

The results of this assessment should alert you to conflicts or disagreements and make you aware of any negative feelings developing among team members. If the assessment indicates a problem, you may want to investigate, both to keep it from growing and to use the information in individual performance appraisals later.

Assessing Member Behavior

To investigate low ratings on the team behavior assessment or to assess member behavior in general, I recommend using the same assessment items. Create another form by listing the behaviors that received lower ratings and, after each, the team members. If you want to use this form to assess member behavior in general, list all of the expected behaviors.

Here is an example with two behaviors for a team with five members:

Team members treat each other with respect and dignity.
    Joan   _____
    William   _____
    Esteban   _____
    Michelle   _____
    Erika   _____

Team members complete action items as scheduled.

Joan	_____
William	_____
Esteban	_____
Michelle	_____
Erika	_____

If there are not many team members, as in this example, it may be easier to set up the assessment form as a table.

	Joan	William	Esteban	Michelle	Erika
Team members treat each other with respect and dignity.					
Team members complete action items as scheduled.					

Distribute this assessment to all team members and ask them to rate the members on each behavior honestly and anonymously. The results should indicate which team members might benefit from a one-on-one with you. You'll also have evidence to put on file for later performance appraisals.

Stages of Team Development

Bruce Tuckman, a psychologist who did research on group dynamics, proposed a model of group development in 1965 that has become the standard. It consists of four stages: *Forming*, *Storming*, *Norming*, and *Performing*. Each stage is characterized by behaviors to be expected in any team.

In the first stage, Forming, the team members meet and share information about themselves. They discuss the purpose and goals of the team and possibly the role that each will play. In this stage they are focused on their new situation.

In the second stage, Storming, the team members cope with the difficulties of their situation and adapt to their responsibilities. They may compete with each other. They may have different opinions and expectations. Conflicts are to be expected.

In the third stage, Norming, the team members begin to work together more effectively as a team. They are able to focus better on developing ways to collaborate and cooperate. They should be showing respect for each other's opinions and differences. The team generally has rules at this stage as well as processes and procedures.

In the fourth stage, Performing, the team members function well together, working as a team. There is a feeling of trust and interdependence. It should be noted that not every team reaches this fourth stage—and that a team that reaches this stage may revert to an earlier stage, especially if one of the members deviates from normal team behavior, if a new member joins the team, or if there is another big change. Exhibit 9-2 shows these stages.

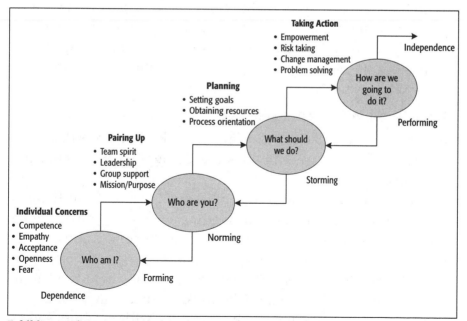

Exhibit 9-2. The Four Stages of Team Development

As mentioned in introducing the Tuckman model of team development, each stage is characterized by behaviors that are to be expected in any team. If you are familiar with the model, you should be mentally prepared for challenges, at least to some extent. As a result, you might want to allow for a few problems and not react to all instances of "bad" behavior—if they are typical for the current stage of the team.

Performance Appraisal of Individual Team Members

At the start of this chapter, I said that when you evaluate the performance of the team you use the team goals as your criteria. I also said you should set *shared* and *individual* objectives for each of the members of the team, to guide performance and to serve as the basis for performance appraisal.

In most situations, it's probably more efficient to add the performance objectives of a team member to his or her other performance objectives and cover them all in a single performance appraisal. However, you might choose to do a separate appraisal process for the team-related objectives, especially if the work of the team ended midway between annual performance appraisals or if the team responsibilities for your employees accounted for most of his or her time and job description.

Team-Centered Performance Review

In addition to the performance appraisal that you do as the team's manager, you may want to consider doing a team-centered performance review.

Consultant Tom Peters and others wrote about the trend of self-managed teams in the 1980s, citing some progressive companies where teams hired and fired their own members and decided on bonuses and pay increases without manager involvement. These were for the most part experiments that were tried in an effort to cut costs by reducing the ranks of first- and second-level supervisors. They produced mixed results, with the more aggressive attempts being rolled back after a few years.

Years later, one of the tools used by self-managed teams, the team-centered performance review, is being tried out for different reasons: no one knows better than the team members how each of them is performing.

You may want to use a peer review as part of your perform-ance appraisal for team employees. Be aware that it's risky to allow peer reviews to carry much weight in performance appraisals. Although it may be true that no one knows better than the team members how each of them is performing, they are also, after working together for any length of time, too close to each other—for better or for worse. Don't expect team members to be fair or even honest in their reviews. If you have your team mem-bers do peer reviews, I'd suggest using the results as just another source of information when you do performance appraisals.

Recognize and Reward Team Achievements ...

By balancing the use of formal recognition (financial and other rewards) and informal recognition (praise and regular feedback), you can reward team members and maintain momentum through-out the process rather than waiting for the team to complete its work.

... and Each Individual

However well your individual employees work together as a team and however much you want to emphasize their collaboration and team spirit, don't forget that employees usually want to be recognized as individuals as well. Psychologist and philosopher William James said, "The deepest principle of human nature is the craving to be appreciated." That's true of your employees. As the authors of *Effective Coaching*, Marshall Cook and Laura Poole say, "Employees take pride in playing on an effective team and share in the reflected glory of a team victory. But that doesn't mean that employees don't appreciate recognition for their indi-vidual efforts and achievement in the team's success. Quite the contrary!" Instead of sending a form memo to "members of the XYZ team," they advise addressing a personal note to the mem-ber, "as long as the notes don't say exactly the same thing." It's most effective to mention "specific, unique behaviors," contribu-tions to the team that recognize the team member as an individual. "Otherwise, even praise seems empty."

Appraise the performance of team members as individuals and recognize them as individuals. That's the bottom line of managing teams and performance appraisal.

A Final Word

Performance appraisals have always been one of the most challenging aspects of a manager's job. Now they are even more challenging with the advent of virtual teams, globalization, economic change, and evolving employee expectations and demands. There is no simple fix, and even the use of technology in structuring the process and improving the modes of communication has not simplified the task.

To conduct the perfect appraisal, the old standards are best:

- Understand what's important to getting the job done from the big picture down to the details.
- Know your people and their abilities, aspirations, challenges, personalities, and needs.
- Plan, plan, plan. Take the time to break down big goals into smaller objectives and ensure that responsibility is fairly apportioned.
- Make the time to observe results and provide feedback.
- Listen more than talk.
- Become the best coach you can be and develop your ability to develop others.

- Evaluate your own managerial performance in terms of how your people are doing. When they are doing well, so are you as a leader.

Index

A

Abilities, 115
Absolutes, avoiding, 70, 91
Accommodators, 142
Achievements, reviewing, 48
Action verbs, 17, 26, 27
Active experimentation, 142
Active listening, 73–74
Adaptability, 32
Age Discrimination in
    Employment Act, 89
Agendas for appraisal meetings,
    55–56, 62
Agendas for coaching sessions,
    156
Aggressive questions, 61
Americans with Disabilities Act
    1990, 89
Analysis-level objectives, 27
Annual appraisals, 83–84
Application-level objectives, 27
Appraisal meetings (see
    Meetings)

Appreciation memos, 100
Aptitudes, 115
    (See also Potential)
Assimilators, 143
Assumptions, avoiding, 102
Attainable goals, 17, 18
Attitude, 83, 120–123
Attribution bias, 51
Auditory learners, 141
Average performance, 52

B

Bacal, Robert, 4, 19, 45–46, 53,
    55, 66, 67, 107, 110, 118, 132,
    135, 162
Balanced evaluations, 53
Balanced scorecards, 11
Barsoux, Jean-Louis, 86–87
Behaviorally anchored rating
    scales, 28–31
Behaviors, focus on, 54, 71,
    82–83, 91
Best employees, starting with,
    47–48

Bias, 49–52
Blaming, avoiding, 77
Blanchard, Ken, 99, 137
Bloom's taxonomy, 26, 27
Body language, 67, 69, 149–150
Bowen, R. Brayton, 99
Brainstorming, 110
Branham, Leigh, 129
Bruce, Anne, 55, 102, 116, 144, 151, 153
Business acumen, 35

C

Call handling skills, 34
Career development (*see* Personal development)
Carrots and sticks, 136
Cause-and-effect diagrams, 112
Central tendency error, 52
Change management skills, 35
Civil Rights Act of 1964, Title VII, 88
Civil Rights Act of 1991, 88
Client consulting skills, 35
Closed questions, 58, 59, 61, 110
Coaching:
    applying penalties, 160–162
    communication in, 138–143
    elements of, 133–135
    feedback in, 150–154
    guidance in, 145–150
    hallmarks of effectiveness, 135–136
    monitoring progress, 155–156
    motivation, 143–144
    new skills or procedures, 154–155
    observation, 135, 137–138
    performance indicators for, 32
    self-evaluation, 164–165
    in sessions, 137, 156–160

(*See also* Performance management)
Collaboration, 25–26, 34
    (*See also* Teams)
Comments on appraisal forms, 53–55
Commitment, 32
Communication in coaching, 138–143
Communication skills, 29–30, 33
Comparisons, avoiding, 50, 71–72, 120
Compensation, 106–107
Competencies
    converting to objectives, 24–26
    defined, 24
    performance indicators for, 25, 29–30, 32–39
Comprehension-level objectives, 27
Computer-based forms, 40–42
Confidentiality, 85
Constructive criticism, 71
Continuous improvement, 132
Convergers, 142–143
Cook, Marshall J., 148, 177
Corporate strategies, 9, 10–11
Credibility, 32
Cross-cultural bias, 49
Customer business knowledge, 36
Customers, feedback from, 14–15

D

Defensiveness, 75
DelPo, Amy, 107
Deming, W. Edwards, 118
Developmental stages of teams, 174–176
Development needs (*see* Personal development)

Diagnoses (*see* Performance diagnosis)
Difficulties (*see* Problems)
Directional questions, 58–59, 61, 110
Directive questions, 73
Disabled employees, evaluating, 90
Disagreements, 75–77, 157
Disciplinary process, 121, 162–164
DISC model, 143
Discrimination, 87–89
Disparate impact, 88
Disparate treatment, 88
Dissatisfiers, 104–106, 144
Distorting evaluations, 52, 85, 90
Divergers, 142
Documentation:
   assembling for meetings, 66
   of coaching sessions, 158–160
   for comments, 53
   by employees for appraisals, 129
   legal considerations, 84–85
Double jacking, 15
Dulye, Linda, 152

E
Economy, Peter, 99
Edmunds, Fritz, 98
Educational objectives, 26, 27
Emotional reactions, 57–58, 74–75
Empathy, 74
Employee assistance programs, 118
Employees:
   anticipating reactions from, 57–58, 74–75
   avoiding comparisons between, 50, 71–72, 120

development needs, 61–63
discussing appraisals with, 68–78
impact of coworkers' problems on, 108
objective-setting by, 9–10, 125–127
performance appraisal responsibilities, 129
preparing for evaluation meetings, 43–46
(*See also* Personal development)
Enthusiasm in coaching, 135, 143
Equal Pay Act of 1963, 88
Equal treatment principle, 83
Error of central tendency, 52
Esteem needs, 103
Evaluation forms (*see* Performance appraisal forms)
Evaluation-level objectives, 27
Expectations, 113, 134–135
Experiential learning styles, 141–143

F
Failure, encouraging, 86–87
Favoritism, avoiding, 86–87
Feedback in coaching, 150–154
"Fill-in-the-blank" questions, 148
Final ratings, 27–31
   (*See also* Ratings)
First impression error, 50–51
Fishbone diagrams, 112
Five Whys technique, 110–112
Flexibility in objectives, 16
Florida Power and Light, 10
Focused questions, 146
Follow-up:
   on attitude problems, 120–123

Follow-up (*continued*):
    for good performance, 97–107
    performance diagnosis
      approaches, 108–112
    performance diagnosis find-
      ings, 112–120
    performance improvement
      planning, 123–125
    performance planning,
      125–127
    personal development plan-
      ning, 127–128
    scheduling next steps, 79,
      95–96
Follow-up questioning, 60–61
Forming stage (team), 174
Forms:
    coaching results, 160
    coaching session, 159
    communication competency,
      29–30
    listening behaviors, 149
    team assessment, 172,
      173–174
    (*See also* Performance
      appraisal forms)
4Ws and 1H method, 22–24
Francis, Jeremy, 62
Francis, Margaret, 5

G
Galatea effect, 134–135
Generalities, avoiding, 54, 71, 91
Goals:
    converting to objectives,
      22–24
    defined, 10
    for performance appraisals, 46
    (*See also* Objectives)
Gorham, Richard, 44, 54
Grote, Richard C., 57, 96

H
Halo effect, 50
Heathfield, Susan M., 101
Herzberg, Frederick, 104, 143
Hierarchy of needs, 102–104,
    119
High-gain questions, 60, 61,
    72–73
High potential error, 50
Holpp, Lawrence, 167
Honesty in coaching, 135–136
Horns effect, 50
Hygiene factors, 104–105

I
Inconsistencies, 91
Individual recognition on teams,
    177–178
Influence, 33
In-groups, 87
Innovation, 33
Intent, impugning, 91
Intentional distortion, 52, 85, 90
Interpersonal relationship skills,
    33
Ishikawa diagrams, 112

J
James, William, 177
Job descriptions:
    providing to employees, 46
    revising, 47, 127
    setting objectives from,
      11–13
Johnson, Alyce, 133
Joiner, Brian L., 167

K
Kaplan, Robert S., 11
Kinesthetic learners, 141
Knowledge-level objectives, 27

Koch, Ed, 153
Kolb model, 141–143

L

Labels, avoiding, 54, 71, 91
Lake Wobegon effect, 51
Language to avoid, 139–140
Late evaluations, 89–90
Learning styles, 141–143
Leaves of absence, 92
Legal issues:
 avoiding problems, 81–87,
  92–93
 common errors, 89–92
 discrimination, 87–89
Liability, limiting, 90
Life issues, 117–118
"Like me" bias, 49, 91
Listening
 in appraisal meetings, 73–74
 while coaching, 148–150, 157
Lombardi, Vince, 151
Lower-level needs, 103–104

M

Malos, Stanley B., 82
Management by walking around,
 137–138
Managers' role in objective-
 setting, 8–9
Manzoni, Jean-François, 86–87
Maslow, Abraham, 102
Maslow's hierarchy of needs,
 102–104, 119
Max, Douglas, 55
McGregor, Douglas, 119
McNamara, Carter, 143
Measurable goals (see Goals;
 Metrics; Objectives)
Meetings:
 closing, 78–79
 coaching, 137, 156–160

discussing evaluations, 68–78
follow-up, 79, 95–96
introductions, 56–57, 67–68
manager preparations, 55–63,
 65–67, 131–132
preparing employees for, 43–46
progress, 18, 126, 155–156
(See also Performance
 appraisals)
Metrics:
 for customer feedback, 15
 in SMART goals, 17
 for strategic goals, 10–11
 for team appraisals, 168–169
Microsoft Word, 41
Mirroring, 49–50
Morale, 102, 144
Mote, Dave, 52
Motivation:
 in coaching, 143–144
 diagnosing problems related
  to, 115–117
 by rewards vs. recognition,
  97–98
 teams, 177–178
 theories, 102–106, 143–144
Motivation-Hygiene Hypothesis,
 104–105, 143–144
Myers-Briggs Type Indicator, 143

N

Narratives on appraisal forms,
 53–55
Needs hierarchy, 102–104, 119
Negative consequences,
 121–122, 161–162
Nelson, Bob, 99, 100
Norming stage (team), 175
Norms, discriminatory, 87–88
Norton, David P., 11
Note taking, 66, 75, 138

O

Objectives:
 from competencies, 24–26
 effectiveness criteria, 16–18
 factors in creating, 10–15
 linking compensation to, 107
 managers' and employees'
  role in setting, 8–10,
  125–127
 motivation and, 106
 purposes, 7–8
 for teams, 168
 writing, 22–24, 26, 27
Observant coaching, 135
One-Minute Manager
 (Blanchard), 99
One-sided conversations, 92
*1001 Ways to Reward
 Employees* (Nelson), 99
On-the-spot coaching, 137
Open communications, 140
Openings for appraisal meetings, 56–57, 67–68
Open questions, 59, 60, 61, 110
Organizational awareness, 36
Organizational strategies, 9,
 10–11
Out-groups, 87
Output measures, 169
Overevaluation, 90

P

Pareto principle, 13
Past performance error, 51
Patience in coaching, 136
Pay for performance, 106–107
Peer reviews, 13–14, 177
Penalizing performance prob-
 lems, 121–122, 161–162
Perception dimension, 141–142
Perceptual modalities, 141

*Perfect Phrases for Documenting
 Employee Performance
 Problems* (Bruce), 55
*Perfect Phrases for Managers
 and Supervisors* (Runion),
 146
*Perfect Phrases for Performance
 Reviews* (Max and Bacal), 55
*Perfect Phrases for Setting
 Performance Goals* (Bacal), 19
Performance appraisal forms:
 common shortcomings, 21–22
 completing, 47–55
 computer-based, 40–42
 focusing discussions on, 70
 objectives sections, 22–23
Performance appraisals:
 basing objectives on, 13
 closing tips, 179–180
 completing evaluation forms,
  47–55
 discussing with employees,
  68–78
 employees' role, 129
 final ratings, 27–31
 goals for, 46
 levels of use, 1–4
 meeting preparations, 55–63,
  65–67
 origins, 5
 potential and, 31–40
 preparing employees for,
  43–46
 procedures, 82
 separating from career development, 62–63, 95–96, 129
 for team members, 176–177
 for teams, 168–174
 technology for, 40–42
 (*See also* Meetings)

Performance diagnosis:
  continuous, 132
  as focus of appraisal, 77–78
  identifying causes and
    solutions, 112–118
  initial steps, 108–112
  of successful work, 119–120
Performance improvement
  planning, 123–125
Performance indicators, 25,
  29–30, 32–39
Performance management:
  applying penalties, 160–162
  coaching sessions, 137,
    156–160
  communications, 138–143
  cycle, 5–6
  disciplinary actions, 162–164
  feedback in, 150–154
  guidance in, 145–150
  monitoring progress, 155–156
  motivation, 143–144
  observation, 137–138
  purposes, 4–5
  scheduling, 131–132
  self-evaluation, 164–165
Performance Management
  Maturity Model, 1–4
Performance planning, 125–127
Performance problems (see
  Problems)
Performing stage (team), 175
Personal development:
  in coaching, 145
  identifying needs, 61–63
  objectives for, 15, 106
  planning, 127–128
  separating from appraisal,
    62–63, 95–96, 129
Personal issues, 117–118, 136
Personal prejudice, 49

Peters, Tom, 176
Physiological needs, 103
Plan-Do-Check-Act cycle, 6
Platinum Rule, 101–102
Pointed questions, 148
Poole, Laura, 148, 177
Position descriptions (see Job
  descriptions)
Positivity in coaching, 135, 147,
  161
Potential, 31–40, 50
Potton, Les, 127
Praise, 99–100
Preference dimensions for
  learning, 141–142
Prejudice, 49
Preparation for performance
  appraisals, 43–46
Presentation skills, 34
Pressure for improvement,
  160–162
Prior appraisals, objectives from,
  13
Priorities, 8, 12–13
Privacy for feedback, 151
Probing questions, 147
Problems:
  diagnosing, 77–78
  importance of confronting,
    85–86
  improvement plans, 123–125
  progressive discipline
    process, 121, 162–164
  in teams, 171
  unfairly creating, 86–87
  (See also Performance
    diagnosis)
Problem solving, 37, 77–78
Procedures for performance
  appraisal, 82 (See also Meetings; Performance appraisals)

Process improvement skills, 37
Processing dimension, 142
Process measures, 169
Procrastination, 89–90
Product knowledge, 37
Progressive discipline process,
    121, 162–164
Progress meetings, 18, 126,
    155–156
Project management skills, 38
Protected leaves, 92
Pygmalion effect, 134

Q
Questions:
    for appraisal meetings, 58–61,
        67, 68, 72–73
    in coaching, 145–148
    for performance diagnosis,
        109–112
    team assessment, 170–171

R
Ratings:
    of coaching skills, 165
    criteria for, 93
    disagreements over, 75–77
    objective, 49
    opening discussions with, 69
    systems for generating, 27–31
    (*See also* Performance
        appraisals)
Reactions from employees,
    57–58, 74–75
Recency effect, 50, 51
Recognition and rewards,
    97–107, 177–178
*Recognizing and Rewarding
    Employees* (Bowen), 99
Reflective observation, 142
Rehabilitation Act of 1973, 89
Relationship building, 33

Relationship management skills,
    36
Relevance of goals, 18
Relevance of questions, 146–147
Reprimands, 121
Research and analysis skills, 38
Resources, problems related to,
    113–114
Respect in coaching, 136
Responsibilities, confusion over,
    113
Rewards and recognition,
    97–107, 177–178
Rhetorical questions, 148
Risk management skills, 38
Runion, Meryl, 55, 146, 154

S
Safety needs, 103
Salaries, 106–107
Satisfiers, 104, 106, 144
Scholtes, Peter R., 167
Segal, Jonathan A., 89
Selden, Bob, 168
Self-actualization needs, 103
Self-evaluations, 45–46,
    164–165
Self-expectations, 134–135
Self-managed teams, 176
Sensitivity in coaching, 135
Service knowledge, 37
Settings for appraisal meetings,
    65–66
Set-up-to-fail syndrome, 86–87
Shared objectives, 168
Silence during conversations, 71
Similarities, bias based on,
    49–50, 91
Skills, defined, 115
Slover, Alan L., 124
SMARTER objectives, 19

SMART objectives, 16–18, 26
Smartphones, 41
Social needs, 103
Software, 40–42
Specificity of feedback, 152
Specificity of goals, 17
Stages of development, team,
    174–176
State fair employment practices
    acts, 88
Stereotyping, 91
Storming stage (team), 174–175
Strategies, aligning objectives
    with, 9, 10–11
Streibel, Barbara J., 167
Stretch objectives, 106
Success, diagnosing, 119–120
Summary ratings, opening with,
    69
Supportive coaching, 135
Surprises, avoiding, 57–58, 66
Surveys:
    employee motivation, 144
    team assessment, 170–171, 172
Synthesis-level objectives, 27
Systems, 114–115, 118–119

T
Tactile learners, 141
The Team Handbook
    (Scholtes/Joiner/Streibel), 167
Teams:
    defined, 167
    developmental stages,
        174–176
    performance appraisals,
        168–174, 176–177
    recognition and rewards,
        177–178
Teamwork, 25–26, 34

Technology for performance
    appraisals, 40–42
Technology skills, 39
Terminations, 121–122, 163–164
Theory X managers, 119
Theory Y managers, 119
360-degree feedback, 13–14
Time commitments for evalua-
    tions, 96
Timeframes:
    evaluation frequency, 83–84
    for evaluation meetings, 44–45
    evaluation periods, 91
    improvement plans, 123
    for objective setting, 18
Title VII, Civil Rights Act of
    1964, 88
Total Quality Management, 118
Training, 124
Transaction processing skills, 39
Tuckman, Bruce, 174
Two-person brainstorming, 110

U
Unintentional discrimination, 88

V
VAK model, 141
Verbal warnings, 121, 163
Visual learners, 141

W
Walsh, David J., 92
Warnings, 121, 163
"What Matters to You?" tool,
    116–117
Words to avoid, 139–140
Work group objectives, 8–9, 11
    (See also Teams)
Workload management skills, 34
Written reprimands, 121, 163

About the Author

Lawrence Holpp has been a leader in human resources and organizational development for over 35 years. Beginning his career with Blessing-White, Larry developed a variety of customized training solutions for clients. At Chubb Insurance, Larry led the management development and new employee orientation efforts for 3 years before going into consulting with Development Dimensions International. At DDI, Larry was instrumental in creating, developing, and delivering their team-based training solutions to dozens of clients. During that time, Larry also published over 18 articles in *Training* magazine, The *ASTD Journal*, and other professional magazines on the subjects of self-directed teams, quality, and change management.

Over the next 10 years, Larry ran his own consulting business under the name of Quality Partners. He initiated and led total quality management programs in nine hospitals and many other client organizations emphasizing both Six Sigma training and leadership and management training to accompany quality renewal. During this time, Larry coauthored the best selling *What Is Six Sigma?* with Pete Pandy and *Managing Teams*, a title in the McGraw-Hill Briefcase Books series.

At GE Capital, Larry was VP of HR for Quality and Organizational Development with the Structured Finance Group, where he was responsible for all GE-mandated training, surveys, employee engagement efforts, and quality. He later joined Fidelity Investments where he served as VP Operations Consulting and led the training, organizational development, and quality efforts for a major division.

Larry is currently consulting with Gartner Consultants, DeLeeuw Consulting, and independently on a wide variety of HR projects including developing a performance management model for Gartner, a manager's HR handbook, several ongoing projects integrating HR best practices with six sigma projects.

Larry resides in Jensen Beach, Florida and Rome, New York.